MANSELL
AND WILLIAMS
The Challenge for the Championship

MANSELL
AND WILLIAMS

The Challenge for the Championship

Nigel Mansell
& Derick Allsop

Photographs by John Townsend

Foreword by Frank Williams

Weidenfeld & Nicolson, London

To my wife, Rosanne, and
everyone at Williams, especially
Frank Williams, Patrick Head and Sheridan Thynne,
for making things possible this year. N.M.

© George Weidenfeld and Nicolson Ltd and Nigel Mansell Services Ltd, 1992

First published in 1992 by George Weidenfeld and Nicolson Ltd,
Orion House, 5 Upper St Martin's Lane, London WC2H 9EA

British Library Cataloguing-in-Publication data
A catalogue record for this book is available from the British Library

ISBN 0 297 83151 8

Design by Behram Kapadia
Typeset by Selwood Systems, Midsomer Norton
Colour separations by Newsele Litho
Printed and bound in Great Britain by Butler & Tanner Ltd, Frome and London

Contents

A lighter moment with Frank Williams, Phoenix, 1991

Previous pages Magny-Cours, 1991, first victory of the season, marked the beginning of the championship trail.

Foreword

*T*he Williams-Mansell relationship is long-standing, very strong and has proved very productive. We know each other very well – a big advantage in this business – and have, over the years, brought out the best in each other. We share a passion for racing, the will to compete and the will to win. Working with Nigel is always stimulating and never dull.

He gave us a much-needed lift when he rejoined us at the end of the 1990 season, and I like to think we provide Nigel with the right environment to deliver the best of himself. He has, after all, won more races in our cars than any other driver. All but three of his Grand Prix successes have been achieved driving for us.

There is no doubt that Nigel has developed and improved with experience. He thinks about his racing and willingly does his Saturday morning homework at the races. All drivers, especially the quicker ones, want to have the best times every session, so it takes courage to say, 'Forget that, let's run on full tanks and get it right for the race.' Nigel understands that is the most important thing and that results have to be worked for.

And then, when he gets in the car, you know he's going to give it everything. That's the way he is. He's exciting and he's a fighter. He's a real racer.

FRANK WILLIAMS
Didcot, Oxfordshire

Introduction

*T*he road to the top was never meant to be easy, but Nigel Mansell's path has been perhaps more arduous than most. The obstacles have come in many and varied guises: limited finances, serious injuries and lingering scepticism. That he has overcome them all to take on the mantle of Britain's leading racing driver and consistent challenger for the Formula One World Championship is testimony not only to his pace and skill but also to his determination and unflinching self-belief. Significant, too, has been the constant support of his wife Rosanne, who agreed to the sale of their home to fund Nigel's early ambition. She shared his conviction, and his will to go on when he broke his neck and then his back.

Their reward was Nigel's test contract with Lotus in 1980, and that year he made his Grand Prix debut in Austria. The following season he became a fully-fledged member of the Formula One cast and, under the guidance of that great impresario, Colin Chapman, began his quest for stardom. After the death of Chapman, in December 1982, however, Nigel's career lost momentum and direction. He needed a fresh start and fresh hope. Williams were prepared to accommodate him on both counts and he joined them for the 1985 season.

Nigel's performances were to exceed their expectations. He achieved his first success that autumn in the Grand Prix of Europe, at Brands Hatch, and immediately followed up with victory in South Africa. In 1986 he won five races and led the Championship for much of its course. Fate, alas, was to deny him the title. He was comfortably holding the third place he required in Adelaide when a rear tyre on his Williams Honda exploded. In 1987 he won six races, twice as many as any other driver, only to be ruled out of the final two rounds through injury, and again he had to settle for the runner-up place.

For 1989 Nigel decided on a change of course, accepting what proved to be the last invitation extended to a driver by Enzo Ferrari. The Englishman responded by giving the legendary Italian team victory first time out, in Brazil. He delivered another, dazzling win in Hungary. He won in Portugal the following season but his planned title campaign never materialized. He felt he had been politically out-manoeuvred by Alain Prost and came to the conclusion there was no point staying at Maranello.

Furthermore, he saw no future for himself in Formula One and, on the evening of the 1990 British Grand Prix, at Silverstone, announced his intention to retire at the end of the season. One man who would not accept that decision was Frank Williams, and he eventually convinced Nigel he

A congratulatory kiss from Rosanne after winning the 1992 Mexican Grand Prix. Her continuing support has been vital

The Lotus days – Austria, 1983

could put him on the Championship trail again. The deal was duly struck. Nigel was back at his spiritual racing home.

The FW14, equipped with a semi-automatic gearbox and powered by a Renault 3.5 litre V10 cylinder engine, had inevitable teething problems, but Nigel's breakthrough came in France, where he surpassed Stirling Moss's English record of 16 Grand Prix wins. An ecstatic Silverstone gallery saw him dominate his home race, and an equally masterful success in Germany made him the first Briton to complete a hat-trick of victories for twenty years. Coincidentally, the last man to accomplish that feat, Jackie Stewart, did so with the same sequence of races.

The Championship, however, was still to be an elusive target for Nigel. Despite further wins in Italy and Spain, he could not make up the ground lost to Ayrton Senna and McLaren Honda, who had run away with the first four Grands Prix of the season. The last lap horror of Canada and the wheelnut catastrophe of Portugal compounded Nigel's frustration and, for the third time in his Formula One career, he ended the season runner-up.

There was, though, considerable consolation for driver, team and Formula One. Mansell and Williams were back in business. They had given McLaren a run for their money and the sport a season to savour. They resolved to redouble their efforts and, in 1992, resume their challenge for the Championship.

DERICK ALLSOP
February 1992

Acknowledgements

This book has been compiled with the help and forbearance of many people, and we would like to express our sincere gratitude to all of them. We are indebted to the entire Canon Williams Team for their co-operation with our project and especially to Frank Williams, Patrick Head, Sheridan Thynne and Peter Windsor for their time and observations. We also wish to thank Sue Allsop, Ann Bradshaw, Jean-Jacques Delaruwiere, Tony Jardine, Rosanne Mansell and Sue Membery for their kind assistance.

A chance to ponder ...

The Man

I have now been in Formula One for twelve years and one question I am regularly asked is, 'How do you maintain your motivation?' I am in no doubt that in 1991, and through to 1992, the driving force was the opportunity to go for the World Championship. This was why I reversed my decision on retirement in 1990 and signed for Canon Williams Renault. Rather than merely going through the motions, they shared my will to compete and to win.

But really to appreciate what makes a racing driver – and certainly this racing driver – go on, you have to understand the background. The possibility of seriously challenging for the Championship did not arise overnight. It came about through years of effort and perseverance, and when a driver actually gets that chance, a real chance, to go for the greatest prize in his sport, he would have to be crazy to throw it away. The chance was there for me, and I was resolved to do my utmost to take it.

I have actually been racing and competing for more than twenty-eight years since I began in karts. It has been my life. It's what I do. I AM a racer. Whenever I get into a car I will commit myself and do everything in my power to achieve the best possible result. All things being equal, that will mean going for the win. Sometimes, though, all things are not equal and a win can be out of reach. Then you go for the best you can. I think it is precisely because I have often had to fight against unequal odds that I have a greater degree of commitment, resilience and determination.

Just how much bravery comes into it I am not really sure and is for other people to judge. But any driver who steps into a racing car takes risks. We have no illusions on that score. This is a dangerous business. I calculate, and there's no question the calculations improve with experience. My instinct is to stand my ground and that, I believe, should be the instinct of any thoroughbred racer. I'm not prepared to be second best unless forced to. When you are forced to, however, you must learn to recognize it and not try anything foolish; in that way you minimize unnecessary risk.

It is unforgivable to offer less than one hundred per cent effort. That is something no professional should be forgiven. Some people who talk about commitment don't really know the first thing about it. If I go to a circuit, especially on race day, and feel that my performance could be impaired in any way I am very disappointed with myself. At the Spanish Grand Prix, in 1991, I'd injured my ankle in a Press football match a couple of nights before the race. I suffered with it for some days after but on race day itself, with the adrenalin pumping, I don't think my performance level was affected

Barcelona, 1992

Above On the waterfront, at home in Florida

Left Playtime for Chloe, Leo and Greg

Nigel and Rosanne in the living room of their Florida home

and I managed to win the race. If ever a professional sportsman has to be questioned about giving of his best, then perhaps that is the time to ask himself whether he should be competing at all.

I am very conscious that we, as drivers, are paid to perform and to entertain. People pay good money to see Formula One motor racing. The races attract big crowds and huge television audiences. Race fans are entitled to value for money and I like to think I give them just that.

A lot is said and written about the contracts of top drivers, much of it way off the mark, I might add. It is true that those at the very top are paid well, and I don't think they should be embarrassed to admit it. I believe they deserve every penny. The top people in other sports also get paid handsomely, and some of the big names in the music and entertainment industry make far more money than racing drivers do. And they don't risk their lives every time they go out to work!

It is a long haul to the top of Formula One and there are no guarantees of success. The climb demands ability, self-belief and often a great deal of sacrifice. I know some people say I work at my driving, that I perhaps don't have the natural instincts of some others, but no-one can do what we do, at our level, purely by working at it. A lot of what we do is done instinctively; it has to be.

I have had to work for the opportunity to use my ability, and that is where self-belief comes in. Had I not had that belief in my ability I could not have battled on through the early days. Fortunately for me, my wife, Rosanne, shared that belief and together we made the sacrifices that were necessary to keep me in racing. Every important decision of my career has been made with her.

I am quite certain that my commitment to the job is a consequence of having had to sacrifice so much in the past. Nothing came easily, nothing was presented on a plate. It is easy for people to forget we once had nothing in the bank and lived in rented accommodation because we had to sell our home in the Midlands. But I remember, I remember all too vividly, and it's no bad thing that I do remember because it helps me retain a healthy perspective and appreciate what I have now. It serves as a reminder of what can be achieved if you really and truly believe you can succeed. If you do not honestly have that belief, you should save yourself the heartache and aggravation because you will never make it to the top.

Even when you have made it to the top of Formula One, it's far from being an easy ride in physical terms. Over the years the cars have become more and more difficult to drive. Although we now have considerably less power than in the days of the turbos, we are still going round some circuits six or seven seconds a lap faster. You don't find that time on the straight, you find it on the corners; and when you are cornering at these increased speeds, you are pulling ever more G-load – as much as lateral 5G at the tightest part of some corners, or five times the force of gravity. Imagine the strain this puts on the neck muscles, with the head and helmet effectively five times their normal weight. The force of acceleration and deceleration is also astonishing, intensifying the strain and demands on the body.

Grand Prix cars are not comfortable. Cockpits are tight and the body can take an incredible battering. Apart from the general shaking, you can finish a race with knees and elbows raw, hands and fingers blistered. I am broad compared with most of the other drivers on the circuit and cannot

Left Cockpits are tight in Grand Prix cars – Brazil, 1992

Above A painful end to another Championship bid – Japan, 1987

actually sit back in my seat with my shoulders flat, which means I have to hunch forward to fit in the car. Apart from the usual discomfort, my body has been subjected to one or two heavy accidents. Having broken my back a couple of times and my neck once, my spinal column and vertebrae have been crushed to the extent that I am now a genuine half- to three-quarters-of-an-inch shorter than I was at the age of twenty-one.

Another disadvantage of being bigger than other drivers is that I instantly forfeit time. Drivers such as Ayrton Senna or Alain Prost, who are several kilos lighter, may gain as much as half a second a lap this way. Unfortunately, drivers in motor racing don't have a weight handicap system as jockeys in horse racing do; the minimum weight applies to the car.

To contain my weight as much as possible and sustain peak fitness means a strict training schedule and diet, especially through the winter months, when the driver must prepare for the coming season. Fine weather facilitates training and this was one of the main considerations when we decided to make our winter base in Florida.

We made a thorough search of the state in the hope of finding the right location and environment for the whole family. We have three young children – Chloe, Leo and Greg – so schooling was a prime factor. We also had to bear in mind the requirements of our two dogs, four cats and tortoise!

We settled for Clearwater, on the Gulf of Mexico. We liked the area, there are lots of beaches, good facilities and we discovered an excellent school. The house is on the highest point along the coast – all of 57 feet above sea level. It was once the site of Fort Harrison. The Floridian-style house needed quite a bit of work doing to it, but it was just the sort of place we were looking for. It also had plenty of garden, which was important for the children and the animals, and it wasn't long before we extended the menagerie. As well as our labradors, Abbey and Kizzy, we now have an Akita, called Bonnie. There are sub-tropical plants, palms and citrus fruit trees in the garden, but we are particularly fond of two large, ancient oaks on the lawns. One is apparently around 470 years old, the other about 370. Down at the bottom of the garden – literally at the bottom of the garden – is the Inner Coastal Waterway, which is sheltered from the ocean by keys. If we want to go boating, fishing, or riding on the jet ski and wet bike, we can do so right there.

From the point of view of my training programme and the general outdoor life I'm sure we made the perfect choice. I think the move has actually presented me with the possibility of extending my career. I find that being in a warmer climate I'm not in half as much pain as I used to be in the cold, damp weather of European winters. In Florida I'm up at half-past six in the morning, ready to work; in Europe I simply couldn't get my body to operate that early.

I try to vary my training as much as possible to achieve a good level of all-round fitness and stamina, as endurance is vitally important in Formula One. I was very happy with my level of fitness in the 1991 season but was determined to be in even better shape for '92, right from the very first race.

As well as devising an effective exercise schedule, I have to make sure I

Opposite The other team ... Nigel with Rosanne, Chloe, Leo, Greg and dogs Kizzy and Abbelina (known as Abbey) in their garden at Clearwater

Below left Rosanne and Nigel in their ballroom

Below centre Records of a different kind in Nigel's den

Below right Business as usual in the office

eat the right things and I don't always find that easy. I am a pudding man by nature, and it takes a lot of will-power to lay off the desserts and ice creams. In America, of course, temptation in the form of hamburgers, fries and food halls is everywhere. On top of that the children raid the 'cookie jar' and, having been brought up to share, they naturally offer one to Dad. It takes a lot of self-discipline to say 'no'.

My average winter day would start with a round of golf at my local club in Clearwater, Belleair Country Club. A brisk one at that. I like to be the first on the tee and get round as quickly as possible. I find it a good way of loosening the body and clearing the mind. I've even got them laying bets at the pro' shop on how quickly I will get round. My record is one hour twenty minutes!

After the golf I'd go back home for breakfast: grapefruit from the garden, cereal and possibly toast. Later in the morning I might do some mountain bike work, which is very good exercise. For lunch I'd have something like a vegetable stir fry. In the afternoon I'd perhaps mix the training 'diet' with some water sports. I've been learning how to handle the jet ski, which isn't easy to start with. It's important not to get bored, so the more fun you can have in the routine, the better.

More serious work comes in the gym: on the cycling machine, rowing machine and weights. Again, though, I have to be conscious of my frame and be careful not to put on too much muscle and upper body bulk because I'll be even less comfortable in the car. After a bowl of soup I might play tennis, or five-a-side football. This varied programme helps build up my stamina and raises my resistance to exhaustion to new thresholds.

Above Nigel takes *Playful Cub* and *Lionheart* (*above left*) out onto the Inner Coastal Waterway, Clearwater

Opposite Nigel and Leo get to grips with their wet bike

Right Driving towards another sporting goal at the nearby Belleair Country Club

The sweat and toil of the Championship challenge. Nigel devises his own training programme.

That takes discipline, but is absolutely necessary, even if friends and others around you are indulging themselves. Keeping away from alcohol is no problem at all, as I haven't really drunk since I was very young. With the decision to turn professional went a farewell to alcohol. I'd be smashed on a couple of glasses of wine, now! My efforts before the 1992 season were rewarded when I stepped onto the scales in South Africa. I weighed 76 kilos, four kilos (almost 9lbs) less than the previous year.

Spending the winter months in Florida is, I'm sure, of great benefit to all the family. Our children all enjoy sport and the outdoor life. The other important point is that I give myself much more to my family during the winter and Florida is a good place to do this. Formula One can, if you are not careful, become all-consuming. You can't help your mind returning to the job, even in the middle of winter, when you are thousands of miles away from your team. I therefore make a deliberate effort to 'switch off' for a time and try to be exclusively a father and husband. When you have three children you have responsibilities some drivers without children, such as Ayrton Senna, don't have. There are football matches to go to, teachers' nights to attend, children to be collected from here, there and everywhere. Any parent will know what I'm talking about.

In America we can, at least, live a fairly normal life, because Formula One drivers are not so well known as they are in other parts of the world. Please don't misunderstand me, I value the relationship with my fans enormously, but I'm sure you can appreciate that it's nice, now and then, to be able to go out as a normal family and not have the children knocked out of the way by people trying to get to me.

The gardens, tennis court and swimming pool at the Mansells' home in Clearwater

We still regard ourselves as being very much an English family, but now the children go to school in Florida we have had to get used to some of the expressions they have been bringing home. Chloe soon discovered the word 'wow' and suddenly everything is 'wow'; Leo learned that it was 'trash' rather than 'rubbish' and 'excuse me' became 'coming through'! We had a little explaining to do when, before Christmas, we went shopping for 'fairy lights'. That inquiry got us some very strange looks. Rosanne also raised a few eyebrows when she asked the butcher for a 'joint'. She didn't have in mind quite what he thought. . . .

We planned the year so that we could spend most of the summer together in Europe, where the majority of races are at that time, the longer American holidays giving the children the opportunity to join me. We still have our links, and our relatives and friends, in England and the Isle of Man. I still have my Isle of Man Special Constable's badge, and no honour has given me more pride than receiving the OBE.

The children obviously take an interest in what I do for a living, but they won't be following in my footsteps. After we arrived in America the two boys had full medicals and their heights were predicted at well over six feet. That means they are going to be too big for competitive racing, and I'm very thankful. The ideal height for a driver is nearer five foot six than six foot. If they show an aptitude for another sport, say golf or tennis, then I'll be happy to encourage them and help them foster that talent. Motor racing has been very good to me and I will always be grateful to the sport, but I really don't think we could go through it all again. When we look back, we wonder how we got through it the first time.

With the family at home on the Isle of Man

Anyone who has children will tell you their biggest worry is the worry of being a parent, and I am no different. When you consider that aspect of life, motor racing and all other things pale into insignificance. I'm very conscious of the strength they can gain from a solid family background and I am aware of the need to lay plans for their future so that, when they go their own way, they will have the best chance we could have given them.

My real ambition is to come through my racing career intact, happy, and as a family unit. That is my first priority. The success we've had has given us security for the future and I hope we'll be able to enjoy it. I do not have to race for financial reasons and I did, after all, announce my retirement in 1990, only for Frank Williams to come along and talk me out of it!

Of course Rosanne looks forward to the day when I do hang up my helmet. We both do. She is apprehensive when I go to work but she and the children are comfortable and she knows what the Championship means to me. We have talked about it from time to time and have kept it under review. Had the opportunity to try for the Championship in 1991 and '92 not presented itself, I wouldn't have been racing in Formula One. When we feel the time is right for me to stop, then I shall do so.

When that time comes, I intend to enjoy a more regular family life and a rather less hectic life in general. Formula One is a global sport, with an intensely demanding race and test programme. On top of that there are other team and sponsors' requirements, plus as many other appearances and engagements as you can reasonably cope with. I have one or two business interests which I hope to develop in my 'retirement'. I am constantly being approached to get involved in this, that or the other venture

Above Isle of Man Special Constable, number 5

Above right 'No honour has given me more pride than receiving the OBE'

and it would be very easy to keep saying 'yes', but my time is limited outside racing and I won't commit myself to anything unless I have a genuine feel for it.

Since I have long had a passion for golf, it is perhaps inevitable that I should have some interests connected with the game. I have accepted the presidency of the new Dartmouth Golf and Country Club, where the setting is superb and the course excellent. I'm particularly pleased to have this sort of involvement in my own country and I intend to play the course as much as possible in the summer months.

My handicap has been fairly reasonable for a few years, but my figures have taken a bit of a bashing in America and I've been playing off six or seven. I'd like to think I could do something about that when I stop racing. I'm not likely to make the professional tour but who knows, maybe I'll be good enough to make the senior tour by the time I'm fifty; though to compete with the pros, even the old pros, you have to be able to beat par and beat it regularly, and that's quite a challenge.

I am ultra-competitive in everything I do. Most top sportsmen and women are, as that has to be an essential part of their make-up. Something else that should, perhaps, be said about well-known sports personalities is that many of them willingly give of their time and effort for charitable causes, far more time and effort than I suspect the general public realize. The problem is, it simply isn't possible to meet every demand, so please be understanding if, unfortunately, the answer occasionally has to be 'no'.

I am often asked if I get drawn into races on the public roads or get frustrated driving in normal traffic. The answer to both parts of the question

Above The People's Hero, France, 1991

is 'no'. Perhaps when I was very young I might have got a little impatient on normal roads, but not now. I am older, wiser and more tolerant, even if some of the antics on public roads astonish me. I think it is fair to say that although I am a natural competitor, I have also learned, with age, experience and maturity, to relax more. I see no point in competing unnecessarily in areas where I should be finding relaxation and enjoyment. I'll always compete in my professional life to the maximum of my ability, but not knowing when to stop is counter-productive.

If this is all beginning to sound like there are two Nigel Mansells, let me assure you, that's not so. Certainly it's not the way I see it, anyway. I feel every professional, not merely in racing or in sport generally, should be able to take time out to wind down. Then, when he returns to the job, he is refreshed and better equipped to commit himself to what has to be done. In my case the job just happens to be driving a Formula One car. I am a normal family man, and out of the car that's all I am. I believe that helps explain why I have such a good rapport with the fans, not only in Britain but all over the world. I'm not some distant, mysterious being, I am someone they can identify with. They also appreciate the fact that I say what I think.

I'm proud of my relationship with the motor racing public and it's very important to me. I try to make as much time for the fans as I can: to sign autographs, pose for pictures or simply chat. Out on the track I try to acknowledge their support and involve them. I love the atmosphere they generate and there's no doubt their support gives me a lift; I hope they feel I reciprocate by giving them a show. I am a calm, composed man, but also an emotional one, and I am moved by the genuine warmth of a racing crowd. During my spell with Ferrari, in the 1989 and '90 seasons, the Italian fans, the *tifosi*, gave me the nickname *Il Leone* – The Lion. It touched

Opposite top Club selection is vital!

Opposite 'Among my souvenirs', Florida

me deeply because it was an indication of how they saw me. The passionate support I received from the fans while I was at Ferrari is an experience I shall never forget.

What the fans, any fans, want to see is a driver who's going to get out there and give everything. That's what I endeavour to do. It's still the same Nigel Mansell, still the normal family man, but in the car, I am a competitor, I am aggressive, I don't care to be pushed around and I aim to win.

Winning calls for a very positive attitude and I'll try to seek passing opportunities wherever and whenever I can as a second chance may never come. I am aware that people talk about my 'bold manoeuvres' but I'm rarely conscious at the time of pulling off something out of the ordinary. I'm simply doing my job, often instinctively. Everything happens so quickly you just sense the chance and seize it.

There are other situations where you might follow another driver for several laps and have to out-think him in order to pass. It may be a narrow track and you may not have the better car. That's when it becomes a battle of wits. You might try to lure your opponent with a feint, or even a double feint. Whatever the build-up, though, the execution is still going to take a lot of nerve. You may have to keep your right foot down, at 200 mph, and commit yourself to a corner realizing that if something goes wrong there'll be nothing you can do about it. Some drivers try to commit themselves in corners like that, but at the last moment, even though the brain is trying to get the right foot to stay down, it somehow comes off the gas and the attempted manoeuvre fails.

Thankfully, it seems I can still manage to pull off one or two passes. Going into the 1992 season, it was encouraging to know several people were still interested in my services. The 1991 Championship had barely finished when I was receiving offers for 1993 and 1994. At that stage I had no idea what I might do a year on and didn't really want to think that far ahead. The Williams team had come a long way in 1991, and I felt that if the Championship was going to happen for me it might be in '92, because of the way the operation was structured. It had all the makings of a big year for us, and I, for my part, wanted to be better prepared, physically and mentally, than ever before.

I was particularly conscious of the importance of making a good start and maintaining form. Consistency and reliability would be all-important. Our intention had to be to look for finishes from every race. I felt that if we could do that we would score and score well. Even after a stuttering start in '91, we managed a total of seven wins – five to me and two to my team-mate, Riccardo Patrese. As a team we got close to McLaren Honda, and I got close enough to Ayrton Senna to ruffle his feathers.

I had been close to the World Championship a couple of times before, during my first spell with Williams. In 1986 I had done what should have been enough, only for a tyre to explode in the last race in Adelaide, and take my title with it. I have had many setbacks in my career but that was the worst moment of all. The following year I again had to settle for the runner-up place after badly injuring my back in qualifying for the Japanese Grand Prix and being obliged to miss the last two races.

We simply didn't have the muscle to compete against McLaren in 1988 because the regulations allowed the continuation of turbos, but in 1991, when I returned to Williams after two years with Ferrari, we were back in business. Again we were runners-up, yet there was a great deal of satisfaction to be gained from the season, not least because we ensured Formula One had a Championship worthy of the name.

Above Breakthrough victory in the 1991 French Grand Prix

Below Britain's previous Grand Prix winner, John Watson

I think I also proved I reversed my decision on retirement for the right reasons, and that my judgement on Williams' potential was accurate. Ferrari tried to tempt me back for 1992, but while I had gained an enormous amount of experience and confidence at Ferrari, and the proposition they made was an attractive one, my commitment was to Williams. They, Renault, Elf and everybody connected with the organization were dedicated to the task of building on what we had achieved in 1991. I said when I came back to Williams that it was a two-year plan and I had no intention of leaving in the middle and allowing someone else to reap the rewards of all the hard work we'd put in together. I was determined to do everything in my power to try and finish the job.

It seemed to me that McLaren and Senna still had to be favourites for the Constructors' and Drivers' Championships. Their record speaks for itself and I felt they probably had something up their sleeve. They were certain to have made another big effort and probably taken another step forward. There were other possible dangers, too. There had been a lot of changes at Ferrari and they couldn't be discounted. Benetton Ford were also capable of coming through and putting themselves in race-winning contention.

Just about everyone appeared to be agreed, however, that McLaren Honda were still the team to beat and I was preparing myself for another mighty battle with the Brazilian. Not that I was discounting Riccardo, or indeed the other McLaren driver, Gerhard Berger. Although I am the No. 1 driver at Williams, we do not start the season with team orders. Both drivers are free to go for wins, which is fair. The situation is reviewed later in the year and, when it reaches a point where only one driver has a realistic chance of challenging for the Championship, the other is instructed to support him.

I was much more confident coming out of the starting blocks for 1992 than I was for 1991. The all-new car of '91 was the tried and trusted car of '92. On a scale of 1 to 10, my confidence level for '92 was seven or eight compared with only about three for '91.

Much as we anticipated, we had our problems early in the '91 season, but the wait had its consolation. My first success of the year, in the French Grand Prix, at Magny-Cours, took me past Stirling Moss's English record of sixteen World Championship race wins. That was a landmark I took great pride in, Stirling's record had stood for thirty years and I'd like to think mine might stand for a similar period. I followed up that victory in France by winning at Silverstone and Hockenheim, giving me my first hat-trick and the first by a British driver for twenty years. By the end of the year my career total of victories was up to twenty-one and, as people were telling me, I was getting within sight of Jim Clark's twenty-five and Jackie Stewart's British record of twenty-seven. Jimmy was one of my heroes and Jackie, of course, held the world record for a long time.

All records are there to be broken and, just as it is very difficult to compare drivers of different eras, so it is very difficult to compare achievements of different eras. Certain things may have been easier, other things harder in the sixties and seventies. I think all these records and achievements deserve to stand alone, although it would give me tremendous professional satisfaction if I could equal the totals of those two great Scots.

It's rather sad that we don't have several British drivers winning Grands Prix the way we used to have. The completion of the 1991 season meant we'd gone more than eight years since any other Brit', apart from myself, had won a race. That Brit', incidentally, was John Watson.

I certainly don't find my position driving 'for Britain' a burden, rather I regard it as a privilege. But I do sincerely hope we have the talent coming through to represent us in Formula One in the future. I've always been confident we have the ability among our young drivers; the danger is that their potential can be blown up out of all proportion and they fall below expectations. It is grossly unfair to put too much pressure on youngsters. They must be allowed the opportunity to develop their skills without undue pressure or attention. The last thing an emerging driver needs is to be labelled the new Moss, or Clark, or Stewart, or Mansell. He must be himself.

Young drivers can help themselves off the circuit as well as on it by co-operating with teams and sponsors. They must learn to conduct themselves in a professional manner and the word 'no' shouldn't be in their vocabulary. I've seen some drivers in their formative years throw away their chance by being difficult to a manufacturer or some other influential concern. It might prove an exhausting ordeal, but equally, it might prove that vital stepping stone.

Politics and diplomacy are unavoidable features of Formula One, but then I'm sure it's much the same in most walks of life. Experience teaches you to be patient and understanding, to listen to the other point of view. I've certainly learnt to bite my tongue far more than I used to, but there are times when it's essential to speak your mind even if it may make you unpopular.

Within a team, the driver, certainly if he is a senior driver, must accept the responsibility to guide and direct. When it comes to the race, he is the one at the sharp end, he is the man expected to compete and bring the car back in one piece. This is a hard, often harsh game. You have to be tough and stand on your own two feet. And it isn't necessarily fair. But for all the politics and 'hassles' which unfortunately accompany modern Formula One, there are still ample consolations. It's still a special feeling to be out there on a race track with a competitive car, racing to your potential. I still get the buzz and excitement. Without it, I simply wouldn't be able to dredge up the enthusiasm to keep training and planning and preparing for more. I've felt for some time that I've deserved the World Championship, but I am not embittered by not having won it. I have never been obsessed with winning the title and I've certainly not felt the need to 'prove' anything to myself or anyone else. The setbacks can be hard to take at the time, but I try to regain my sense of perspective as quickly as possible. There really are other more important things in life to redress the balance.

It has long been suggested I was fated not to win the Championship, but I sincerely believe fate doesn't come into it. Even after the many misfortunes I have had to endure, I am convinced you can make much of your own luck in Formula One. There's no magic to success at this level, it's all very logical. It comes down to your package. The driver is the wrapping paper around the package. Inside that package he must have the team, the resources and the equipment to give him a genuine chance of competing with the very best in the business. That package must be complete if the man in the cockpit is to have a hope of winning a World Championship. After that it is down to the driver to present the package by driving at the top of his ability and maintaining that standard through a season of varying conditions, climates and circuits.

When I returned to Williams for 1991, I felt that I drove as well as, if not better than, I had done at any time in my Formula One career. I perhaps pushed a little too hard in Japan, where I went off at the end of the straight, but then I had little choice because we needed to win to stay in the

Championship, and I didn't bargain for a sudden problem with the brakes. I honestly believe I had a great year and I think most observers arrived at the same conclusion. The result, as I said earlier, was a contest that held the public's attention virtually to the end.

Had it not been for the odd calamity – Canada, where my car stopped on the last lap after leading from the first corner; Portugal, where a wheel came off following a pit stop and I was later disqualified; and also Belgium, where I had to pull up while in the lead – we might well have made it to the title that season. Even so, there were lots of positives for us to draw strength and inspiration from and there was no reason to be down-hearted or despondent. We had probably exceeded general expectations, and I think Ayrton was a pretty relieved man at the end of it all. He'd won the first four races and looked to have the Championship in his pocket, and was perhaps not anticipating such a strong challenge. I had no problem congratulating him on his third title after the race at Suzuka, but I could already see 1992 and I hoped to give him an even bigger fright. I suspect he sensed that, too.

Throughout the following winter, through the training and the testing, I was focused on the Championship. I have already discussed my long-term goal, but going into the '92 season there was no doubt about my immediate priority – and that was to try and get the Championship job finished. I knew what had to be done, and the team knew what had to be done. Mansell, his 'Red Five' car, and Williams were ready for the challenge.

The crucial 1992 pre-season Estoril test of the FW14B

The Team

*T*he Formula One season may run from March to November, but for the teams there is really no such thing as a closed season. Beneath the huge cooling towers, at Williams' Didcot factory, work goes on round the year. There is inevitably a slight lull in terms of the pressure and tension after the last race and this is when most of the team take a well-earned holiday. The production line never comes to a standstill, though. There are always new parts to be made, new strategies to be discussed, new avenues to be explored. Constant awareness and the ability to stay one step ahead are vital. This is what it takes to succeed in Formula One, and Williams are one of the most successful teams in the business.

They have come a long way since the mid-seventies, when they struggled merely to survive. They were teetering on the edge of bankruptcy, and Frank Williams had to conduct business from a public 'phone box after his own 'phones were cut off. It all changed for the better after Frank linked up with Patrick Head, and Williams Grand Prix Engineering was formed in 1977.

Frank and Patrick have since established themselves as two of the outstanding figures in Formula One: Frank the thrusting, forceful leader; Patrick the brilliant, imaginative designer. Their partnership has endured and prospered, where others have wilted and broken up. Starting with their double Championship victory in 1980, they had won four Constructors' titles and three drivers' crowns, a record of achievement second only to McLaren's in modern times, going into the 1992 season.

It is a measure of the expertise and organization within Frank's team that it was able to continue functioning so well after his terrible accident, in 1986, which left him confined to a wheel-chair. Williams is a thoroughly professional concern, with highly talented personnel and the will to win motor races. Frank is managing director, Patrick technical director and Sheridan Thynne commercial director, all effectively heading separate departments. Frank's team manager is Peter Windsor, his factory manager David Williams (no relation); Patrick works in conjunction with chief designer Adrian Newey; Sheridan is assisted by commercial executives Gary Crumpler and David Owen, and works closely with our sponsorship and PR partners, CSS. Williams currently employs around 180 people.

Team in waiting, Brazil, 1992

Unsung heroes ... work on the
production line at the Williams factory
never comes to a halt

Frank, Patrick and other team members monitor Nigel's progress

Below With team manager Peter Windsor, Hungary, 1991

The present factory, in Basil Hill Road, was opened in 1984 by Michael Heseltine, MP for Henley-on-Thames and then Minister of Defence. Over the subsequent years it has been extended and enhanced, even incorporating a conference centre and museum, where past Williams cars are on display. The factory is a magnificent, hi-tech facility, equipped with the most sophisticated machinery. There is a large new research and development building, and a half-scale wind tunnel, which plays a critical part in determining the design and aerodynamics of the car.

All this super equipment costs money, of course; so does our extensive race and test programme. Formula One is an enormously expensive business, especially if you intend to compete at the highest level. I'm not sure that any team will tell you exactly what their budget is, but Frank will tell you that for 1992 ours was between £20m and £30m. That is an awful lot of money and perhaps more than most teams spend, but it may be rather less than McLaren and Ferrari have at their disposal.

Some people criticize Formula One for the amounts of money poured into the racing of twenty-six cars every other week, but it is an immensely popular spectacle which ranks alongside the Olympic Games and the football World Cup. Unlike those other two events, which are held every four years, Grand Prix racing runs over a nine-month period, every year, and its television audience is measured in billions. The other point which should be remembered, of course, is that Grand Prix racing is a valuable engineering and technological test bed for the automobile industry and a whole range of related industries. Much of what is achieved in Formula One ultimately benefits the man in the street.

The chief source of income for the teams is sponsorship, and the man responsible for bringing sponsorship to Williams is Sheridan Thynne. His strategy is to target potential sponsors carefully, working out which companies might expect to benefit from an association, rather than go chasing companies at random. Canon have been our principal backers for several years and as such earn the right to be incorporated in the official team name, hence, Canon Williams. Unlike many teams, Williams has a number of major sponsors and their contribution to the budget is reflected by their space and position on the car. The other major sponsors are, currently, Camel, Labatt's, Elf and Renault.

Elf and Renault are obviously rather more than sponsors, they are, in fact, partners. Williams designs and produces the car, but two other major pieces of the jigsaw, the engine and fuel, are supplied by the two French companies, Renault and Elf. Renault were pioneers of the turbo-charged engine and I worked with them during my time at Lotus. They pulled out of Formula One at the end of the 1986 season but returned in tandem with Williams for the start of a new normally aspirated era in 1989. They had a couple of wins in each of their first two seasons together and set their sights on greater things from 1991.

Renault's Formula One base is at Viry-Chatillon, some 30 km south of Paris, where they employ 150 people. They provide 50 new engines a year to Williams, plus a number of rebuilt engines. Renault's V10 produces more than 700 bhp and every bit of that muscle is required to have a hope of competing effectively.

Vital extra horsepower can be gained from the fuel, and this has been an area of significant development over the past year or two, so much so that there has been what amounts to open warfare on fuels, fuel chemicals and additives. There are some special petrols around now which give another 60 horsepower or even more; Elf made a big step forward in 1991 only

Below The look of a winner. At the Estoril test of the FW14B, February 1992.

Left The power behind the glory …
Renault's V10 engine

Below Renault Sport's base at Viry-
Chatillon

Opposite Work on engine development is
continuous

Opposite below Renault personnel follow
Nigel's every move

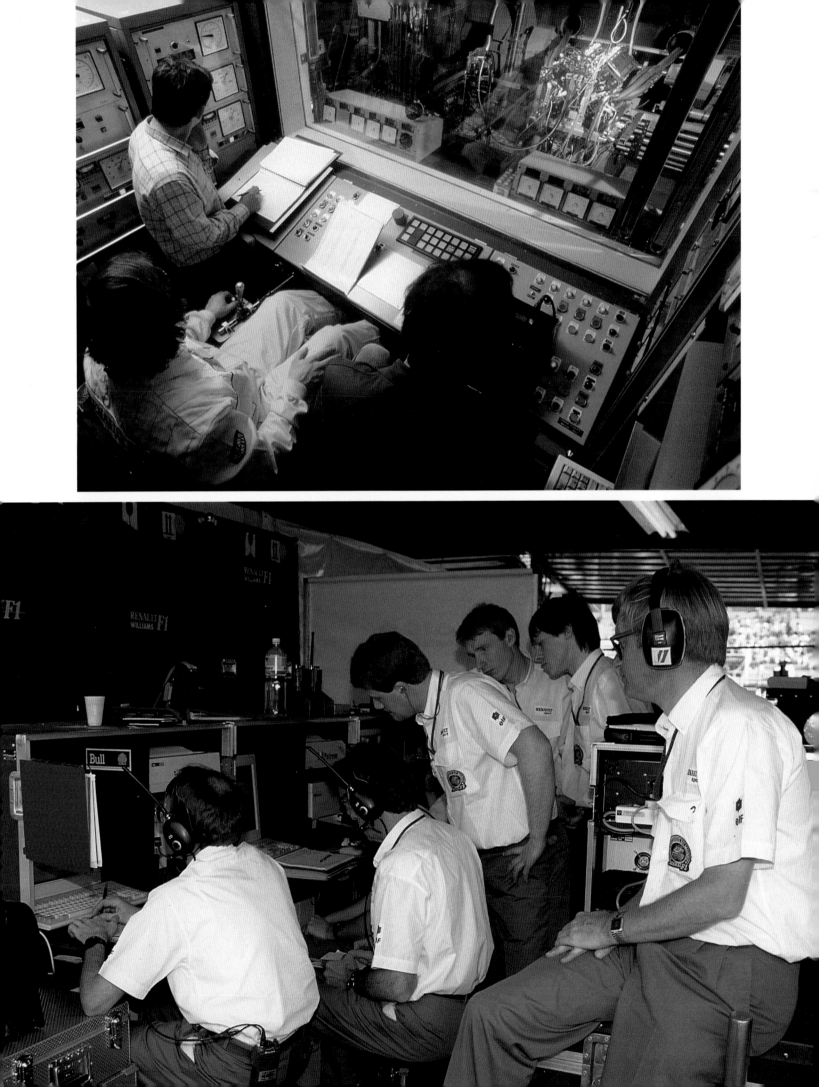

for Shell, who supply McLaren Honda, to respond with an even greater improvement.

The competitiveness in the area of fuel has now created a rather disturbing situation in the sport. I am by no means alone in believing some of these fuels are dangerous; they are very volatile and, so far, the attempts to bring in regulations to control them haven't really worked out. FISA, the sport's governing body, have declared their wish to regulate fuels, but the companies seem reluctant to reach an agreement. Each company believes it is ahead of its competitors and doesn't want to jeopardize that position. It is arguable that FISA should therefore insist that normal pump fuel is used, but unfortunately the situation cannot be resolved that simply, because of the overriding fear that it would cause the fuel companies to pull out, thereby denying the sport billions of dollars of income which it would be almost impossible to replace. The situation is a delicate one, but to fail to address it as soon as possible can only deepen the problem.

This is a good illustration of where motor racing, particularly Formula One motor racing, differs from most other sports. It is big, big business, companies invest huge amounts and look for a return on their investment. That return comes with success and exposure, so competition is inevitably fierce. With a scenario like this the politics are bound to be complex. Formula One is a hard, serious world. Having said that, there are a lot of good, sincere people and companies involved, who really do care about the

Elf set up their own field laboratory at the circuit. Valérie Jorquera of the technical department.

sport as well as their egos and balance sheets. Goodyear is one such company which springs to mind. Goodyear is, I think, THE greatest name in racing tyres. I certainly owe them an awful lot and I believe they deserve the gratitude of racing as a whole. They have been a great, loyal supplier and sponsor for many, many years. They have dominated Formula One in recent years and, following the withdrawal of Pirelli, found themselves supplying the whole field for 1992.

While the engines, fuels and tyres are supplied from outside, the car itself is created at Williams. This is Patrick Head's domain. There can be no doubt that Patrick is one of the greatest engineers and designers ever to test his ingenuity in Grand Prix motor racing. Since the death of Colin Chapman, the two men who stand out are John Barnard and Patrick. It is not just Patrick's record of success which distinguishes him, it is also his record of building strong, safe cars. No matter who you are or which team you drive for, the chances are you are going to have some form of shunt at sometime. I find it very comforting to know I am in one of Patrick's cars because I know it is not going to fall apart on the merest of impacts.

You'll often hear those in Formula One talking about the 'package' because it is the combination of all these essential elements – car, engine, fuel, tyres and, of course, team and driver – which will determine performance and results. If you are weak in any department you cannot expect to come out on top. Williams presented their package to me after I announced my intention to retire in 1990. They had had, by their standards, three modest seasons but were convinced they were about to turn the corner. I listened. Frank was very persistent, and very persuasive. He, Patrick and Adrian Newey were very optimistic about the prospects of their car for 1991, the FW14, which would be totally new. They were pressing ahead with a semi-automatic gearbox and an active suspension system. It is no secret that I had not been happy with Williams' earlier 'active' venture and that was thankfully abandoned during the 1988 British Grand Prix

Above and below Goodyear supply tyres to all the teams in Formula One

Right Behind the scenes at a race weekend

Smiles all round for (*left to right*) Patrick Head, Nigel and Adrian Newey after winning in Mexico, 1992

weekend. (Second place in that race justified the decision and was due reward for a fantastic team effort in converting the car overnight.)

The new version was still some way off but the six-speed, semi-automatic gearbox was well down the road. I had used a seven-speed, semi-automatic transmission at Ferrari and knew there were some tracks where it was an advantage to keep both hands on the wheel at all times. It is not, however, an enormous advantage and, clearly, the more complicated you make your equipment, the greater the risk of problems. Reliability, as we were to be reminded, is a key factor. What impressed me, though, was that Williams was looking to take a genuine step forward. Formula One is so competitive it can change from race to race. If you stand still you go backwards, as Ferrari discovered to their cost in '91. They had finished the '90 season looking strong and seemingly tested well that winter, but took the conservative route, changed very little, and, to their dismay, found themselves trailing badly behind McLaren and Williams when the real action started.

The Williams new 'box still had to be tested during the winter before a final decision was made, but there was a clear commitment to be bold and to be positive. There was also a pledge to give me outright No.1 status in the team, with first call on the spare car, and appoint Riccardo Patrese as my No. 2. I had worked with him in 1988 and regarded him as one of the best team-mates I had ever had. Some people appeared to be surprised that he had such a good spell in 1991, but it didn't surprise me. He can be very quick and is, after all, the most experienced driver in the history of Formula One, with well over two hundred races to his credit, and you don't achieve that without ability. Frank topped up the package by assuring me he was

Team-mate Riccardo Patrese

confident Renault and Elf, too, were prepared to put in the effort and resources required to give us a realistic chance. It all added up to the sort of opportunity I had always wanted, and now it was mine for the taking.

I would also be coming 'home' as I had enjoyed my most successful period at Williams, winning thirteen races. I loved most of my time at Ferrari, and I shall return to that subject later in the book, but, even though I had Italian lessons and managed to get by in general conversation, communication on a technical level was a problem, and everyone has heard about the Ferrari brand of politics. The thought of removing the language barrier and linking up again with people I knew made Williams' offer all the more enticing. One factor which did not influence my thinking was the money. I could have earned far more by staying at Ferrari.

There were many other offers on the table: from Formula One, from sportscars and from American Indycar teams. Some of them were very attractive and I thought about them long and hard. But I was thinking more and more about the Williams' offer, and the pleas from fans and racing people alike to stay in Formula One. Letters arrived by the sackful and as I have always treasured my relationship with the fans, not only in this country but all over the world, there's no doubt they helped sway my decision. What really clinched it, however, was a little stroll one evening with Rosanne. She could sense I wanted to race on and said that if I did I might as well stay in a formula and environment I knew. That meant Formula One, and it meant going back to Williams.

The reaction I got at Williams after signing was tremendously encouraging. Frank said I had given them a lift and I could sense it when I visited the factory, but they did the same for me. There is no better feeling for a driver than to have the support and backing of everyone in the team. If we were going to make the sort of progress we hoped for we had to be united, we had to be pulling together and it would have to be a team effort. Williams had proved in the past that they had the calibre and character needed to succeed, and it was obvious they had the old hunger to do so again. The significance of the TEAM effort cannot be over-stressed. It doesn't matter how good the driver is, he must have the equipment and the backing to produce his best and Williams were determined to give me that.

That first winter back with Williams gave me and the team exactly the impetus we were looking for. They had not had particularly good results with the car during the 1990 season, but we managed to make fairly significant improvements in our lap times in testing. The big leap came at the Paul Ricard circuit, in the South of France. The car was handling like a bus through some corners, so we had a long discussion about possible ways of improving it. I suggested one or two small changes and we tried it again. The difference was incredible and the times tumbled – and this was the old car. If our projected figures for the new car were anything like accurate we were going to be in pretty good shape.

We also used the semi-automatic gearbox and that, too, went pretty well. I had an open mind about that and the active suspension system; if they worked, I wanted them, but without reliability they would not help us. Both these devices are computer-controlled, so many things can go wrong and, when they do, it's particularly frustrating. In our game you have to accept breakdowns, mechanical failures and even wheels falling off! That's motor racing. But a computer malfunction is not what I call motor racing and I

Comparing notes with David Brown and Adrian Newey

am a little disturbed by the computer trend because so much is taken out of the hands of the driver as a result. There is an awful danger that he will become the prisoner of the computer, chained in his tiny cockpit, with no control over his destiny.

As it was, Williams acknowledged there was still work to be done on the active suspension, but the 1991 World Championship car, the FW14, would be equipped with the six-speed, semi-automatic gearbox. The driver selects the gears by pressing two small levers on the back of the steering wheel, one of them to change up, the other to change down. Once he's made his selection, it's over to the computer. If all goes well, it will engage the desired gear, but if the computer plays up, the driver is helpless. You could find yourself going into a corner, selecting second and jumping into fifth.

As with all innovations, the system had to be tried and tested, and we were conscious that the new season was almost upon us. With a new gearbox and a totally new car, teething problems would be inevitable. What made matters worse from our point of view was the change in the points scoring system that season. A win would be rewarded with ten points, instead of nine, which was fair enough, but points from all sixteen races, rather than the best eleven scores, would count towards the Championship. So suddenly it became even more of a reliability Championship than a performance Championship.

For all that, we were committed to the new box and there's no doubt that all Formula One teams are looking down the semi-automatic road. McLaren were working on theirs but were some way behind us at the time. The FW14 was unveiled at a cold, wet Silverstone and I gave it a suitable

Small levers behind the steering wheel operate the semi-automatic gearbox

baptism in a bath of mud! We were left with rather less time to test than we would have liked before the first race, at Pheonix, but the feeling inside the camp was that this was a car worth waiting for. We were optimistic it would soon be pushing its distinctive dolphin-like snout through the Grand Prix fields.

I doubt whether most people appreciate what a long and complex operation is involved in the building of a Grand Prix car, let alone a winning Grand Prix car. Williams is fortunate to have the facilities, resources and ability required. Patrick heads a team of highly-skilled and dedicated engineers and designers. Adrian Newey plays an extremely important role; he is one of the most talented aerodynamicists to emerge in recent years and made his mark with the Leyton House March team. He has had a considerable influence on the design of our chassis.

The drawing office still exists, but beyond that the process of designing a Grand Prix car becomes highly sophisticated and, inevitably, computerized. The wind tunnel is now a familiar feature of the Formula One factory.

The FW14 has its baptism at Silverstone in February, 1991

Chief designer Adrian Newey

Wind flows and scale models of the car are used to simulate conditions on the circuits, and thereby guide the team towards the optimum aerodynamic package. Most teams have quarter scale models, but we now have half scale, which should make our figures even more accurate. Another now widely-used aid to car design is the CAD/CAM facility, which gives pictures of the chassis on a computer screen, enabling the team to assess the effect of small yet potentially important alterations.

Formula One cars used to be made from aluminium alloy sheets, now we use carbon composite materials pioneered in the aircraft industry. These materials are not only much stronger than aluminium, they are also lighter. Up to twenty-four layers are moulded, at varying angles, into the 'tub', which is effectively the driver's safety capsule. FISA regulations require teams to put their cars through ever-more stringent crash tests.

The governing body's regulations relating to the design of cars have been changed constantly over the years in the endeavour to contain speeds and further improve safety standards. In that respect they have generally been very successful and these days we accept it as the norm when a driver walks away unscathed from a big shunt. Bits and pieces of bodywork may fly all over the place and it looks very dramatic, but hopefully the tub will have stayed intact and protected the driver.

The idea that Formula One is now safe is at best misguided. A lot of drivers have been extremely lucky to walk away from horrific accidents, and the luck could swing like a pendulum. It worries me that people think they are indestructible, that they can't get hurt. That is exactly when they do get hurt because complacency can set in. If people are completely fearless, and don't respect the cars they drive, they can cause problems for other drivers, as well as themselves. You can get killed on the road at 30 mph; we're doing more than 200!

Changes in rules have meant, in some cases, drastic changes to the cars, and I feel privileged that in my Formula One career I have gone through so many different eras: ground effect, flat bottoms, turbos and then the return to normally aspirated engines. It has been a tremendous experience driving and competing with such varied cars and engines.

Limits imposed by the regulations have tested the mental agility of the designers. It has become far more difficult to come up with a really significant technical breakthrough because there are so many restrictions. That is why John Barnard was determined to pursue his semi-automatic gearbox project at Ferrari, and why Patrick has done so at Williams. Patrick felt the next area which offered potential for development was the suspension. I'll let Patrick explain the principles and aims of his active suspension system:

'All the current type of Grand Prix cars are very sensitive, aerodynamically, to attitude and ride height. With a conventional, passive suspension system, with coil springs, the ride height and attitude is related to the load on the suspension, and that increases as the car goes faster. That's why the car goes lower when it goes faster, and why you tend to see all those sparks as it goes down the straight. That's when the car is at its fastest.

'There are advantages in running the car fairly low at low speed, so in order to be able to carry the load at high speed it means we have to run pretty stiff springs, which is why the cars tend to leap about over the bumps. So it's a huge compromise in that we are not as low as we would like to be at low speed, but we're really lower than we'd like to be at high speed.

'What we are trying to do, therefore, is overcome that by separating the

Opposite and below The first outing of the FW14B at the Estoril test, February 1992

load-bearing capability of the suspension and its displacement. By having a hydraulic loading system which feeds hydraulic oil, under pressure, into the system, or out of the system, we can have a reasonable degree of control over the attitude and the ride height. Certain fundamentals of this system are similar to our previous system, but the control, the strategy and the way the components are arranged on the car, and the various safety mechanisms that cater for different types of failure, are built into it now. So it's really a much more sophisticated version of the system we had in '88.

'I certainly think it will be a step forward, if not necessarily a major step forward. But, as with all these things, it's a question of whether the advantage of it, which should be better performance, is outweighed by the fact that, statistically, because it's more complicated, it has to be less reliable.'

Just to give an indication of the variations with a passive system, a stationary car probably has a ride height of between 30mm and 40 mm at the front and, say, 50 to 65mm at the back. At speed, the ride height can go down to something like 12mm at the front and 8 to 10mm at the back. The purpose of the active suspension, if the computer is working correctly, is to achieve optimum performance in slow, medium and high speed corners. The aim, in a nutshell, is to sustain speed.

The active system was, naturally, the focus of our attention during 1991-92 winter testing. I had originally planned to take a break in December, while we were settling into our new home in Florida, but in the early part of the month we had a test in Barcelona which was to determine our direction for '92 – and that included a final decision on the suspension. It was imperative, therefore, for me to be there and have some say in the decision-making process. We had two active cars there, which I drove back-to-back for the first three days of the test and Riccardo drove on the final two days. We also had a passive car, which our test driver, Damon Hill, drove.

Below right View of the cockpit of the FW13B

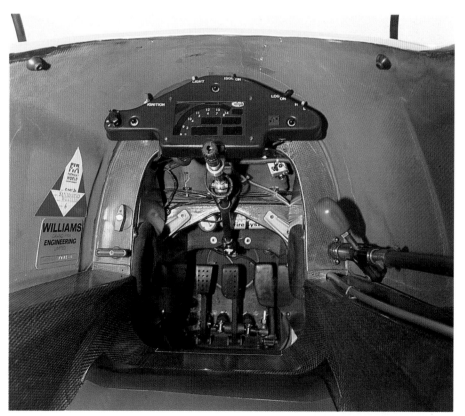

Unfortunately the elements conspired against us and I wasn't able to do as much running as I would have liked. It was bitterly cold on the first day and pouring with rain on the second and third days. We had one or two hiccups we could have done without, but we could see the potential and, when Patrick and I flew back to England to meet Frank, we came to the conclusion that we should go with it. That decision was confirmed publicly after an unprecedented seven-day test at Estoril at the end of February. We even had the race team, rather than the test team down there, and that operation gave us the impetus we needed going in to the first race.

McLaren-Honda-Shell was still the package we would have to beat. Honda and Shell had demonstrated in '91 that they could respond to Renault and Elf, and we felt that if we had a wild card it might be our chassis. We would have some aerodynamic changes, and we could have active suspension. As Patrick has explained, we accepted there could be problems, but we had to try because this was something the competition hadn't got and, if it worked, it just might tilt the balance.

There was a lot of work still to be done on the active suspension, not least to try and reduce its weight, so the rest of the test schedule that winter was going to be crucial. Testing can be extremely productive, or a complete waste of time, and time is priceless. Whatever you are developing – the chassis, engine, gearbox – you can waste an awful lot of money and that money can be replaced, but you can't turn back the clock. The time expended on going down the wrong path is gone forever, so it's of paramount importance that a full and proper assessment is made before choosing a direction.

Some teams go testing just because McLaren, or Ferrari or Williams or some other team are testing, but if they have nothing to test they shouldn't waste their time and money. They should stay at home and try to develop something which might improve their performance. There's only so much a driver can do. He can set up the car, he can drive it as fast as he can, but if it does not have the potential and the engine does not have the horsepower to do the job, his chances of success are minimal.

Testing can be very demanding, as well as time-consuming. Williams has something like twenty-six or twenty-seven tests a year, on top of the sixteen races, with their practice and qualifying sessions, which take the team to just about every corner of the world. Clearly it would be an impossible burden for the same drivers and mechanics to undertake all those duties. While Riccardo and I share the responsibilities where we can, we have Damon Hill as our test driver, and we have a test team.

The test driver is a very important member of the team and we are fortunate to have in Damon an outstanding test driver. He's done a super job for us. He's quick, but he's also sensible, keeps the car on the road and brings back valuable information. Test driving can be hard, monotonous work. Driving from nine to five is very wearing, but it could be the first step in Formula One. I started as a test driver for Lotus and hopefully Damon, who is, of course, the son of the late Graham Hill, will, in due course establish himself in Grand Prix racing.

It is necessary to have someone taking some of the pressure off the race driver because a lot of testing can actually de-tune him. The test driver will be employed to test the life of various parts and do the endurance work, and Damon has undertaken a lot of work with the active suspension and other important developments. Ideally, the race drivers will concentrate on the performance testing. Sometimes the test team can be on the road at the same time as the racing team. While I was winning the 1991 British Grand

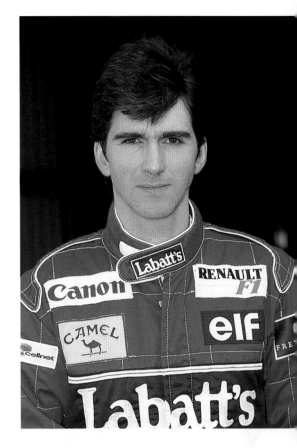

Test driver Damon Hill

Opposite above 'There was still an awful lot of work to be done'

Opposite below With Damon Hill and Press Officer Ann Bradshaw in the Williams truck at the Silverstone test, April 1992

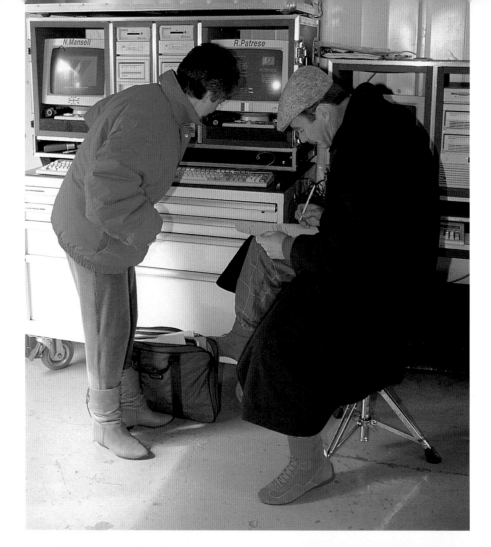

Testing in the UK presents a rare
opportunity to catch up on admin with
PA Sue Membery

The spare car has its own set of
mechanics. Thanking Bob Davies,
number one mechanic, after taking pole
position for the 1992 South African
Grand Prix.

Setting up the car is a compromise – suggesting an adjustment to the ride-height of the car, Silverstone test, April 1992

Prix at Silverstone, a transporter was on its way to Germany for the test at Hockenheim. The schedule in modern Formula One is incredibly hectic and the effort constant.

If tests are planned and utilized correctly, a team can take mammoth steps during what has become an even shorter winter break. Look, for instance, at how Williams bounced back to become very serious and genuine front-runners in '91. In a few months we turned the team around and returned to Championship contention. The car was radically different, but there was a huge effort from all concerned, and the drivers played a part too. A lot of teams have this capability if only time and money are spent wisely, the right direction is chosen and the personnel are suitably motivated.

The entire workforce has to share this motivation, which is absolutely critical at this level of the sport. They must have a true, deep will to succeed and be prepared to try and try again if they don't succeed the first time. With that level of commitment the occasional slip-up is acceptable, difficult though it may be at the time. I have no problem with people who try hard and get it wrong, it's people who don't try hard that I have no time for. But of course what you're really looking for is to ensure that the entire team has proper guidance so that their endeavours are channelled productively.

Teamwork is a basic and essential strength of Williams, and Williams is what I call a real racing team. They are racers through and through, and, judging by the very little turnover in personnel we have, people seem to like the atmosphere within the team and the factory. The mechanics from '91 stayed on for '92.

Grand Prix racing is a tough business. It puts tremendous pressure on its participants' private lives. We are away from home for much of the year, and that can put a strain on relationships, so I think it says a lot for our team that it is as solid and stable as it is. That solidarity and stability can only serve to strengthen Williams further.

Race Weekend

A race weekend usually comprises two days of practice and qualifying sessions, followed by a final warm-up and the Grand Prix itself on race day. It sounds simple and straight-forward, but race weekend for any team is a high-pressure, meticulously planned, finely-tuned operation and only the climax of a complex logistical exercise spreading back for weeks. Organization is a crucial factor in Formula One, and those teams who get the campaign of action right are likely to be the ones out on the main field of battle.

I have the whole season pretty well mapped out at the beginning of the year, and the same goes for the team. Travel arrangements and hotel bookings are made well in advance as flights and rooms are at a premium. I had my own plane for a time but sold it when we decided to winter in Florida. It was outdistanced by the move so now, when we go trans-Atlantic, we usually fly with British Airways. We tend to spend the summer in Europe, much of it on the road with a Renault Espace, which is perfect when I have the family with me.

Formula One is a moving village. The mode of transport for the cars and equipment to races depends on the destination. In Europe, we use our own trucks; for long-haul trips we package everything to be carried on flights organized by the Formula One Constructors' Association. We presently have ten races in Europe, six outside. If we have two long-haul races back-to-back, as sometimes happens with the Americas, a convoy of huge trucks may be arranged to carry the equipment from one venue to the next.

For the races outside Europe preparation begins six or even eight weeks before freight-time. We have to strike a sensible balance in that we must ensure we have sufficient equipment, parts and so on, to do the job properly, but at the same time we must be weight-conscious and not take more than we would reasonably expect to be necessary. It is the same with personnel. Cost and efficiency are always important considerations, and in this regard Williams are probably less lavish than one or two other teams. All the packing is done in one part of the factory and each item is carefully labelled; it is then transported in what we call 'pack horses' to Heathrow.

Transporters line up for the 1991 French
Grand Prix weekend

Above 'I had my own plane for a time'

Below The Renault Espace is ideal for transporting the whole family.

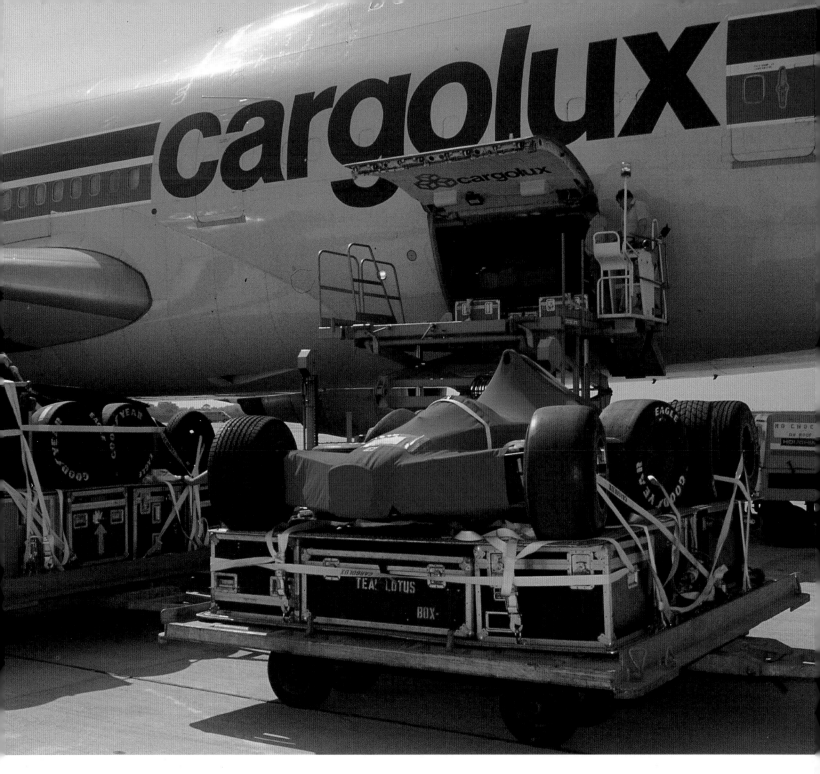

Above Formula One cars on their way to
another race

The truck for European races is not merely a transporter, it is also a
mobile factory and will be a hive of activity over the race weekend. The
truck will set off up to three days ahead of the rest of the team, depending,
obviously, on how far it has to travel. At the circuit, it will reverse up to the
back of the garage which will be our base and stay there until the end of
the event.

For the long-haul races, drivers and other members of the team might
arrive two or three days in advance of first practice to acclimatize and
beat the jet-lag. We are, remember, crossing several time zones, perhaps
switching from very different climates, environments, cultures and even
altitudes and a couple of days relaxing, swimming, playing some golf or
tennis is essential. Once we are in Europe, which is the Championship
scene for the bulk of the summer months, the routine is rather simpler. We
also, for instance, have our own motorhome for the European races, whereas

Left and opposite Shark-fishing in Australia on a free day

elsewhere we have the use of small rooms, caravans or portakabins.

If we are at a new Grand Prix circuit, we would actually start practice on the Thursday before the Sunday race to help 'familiarization'; the driver then has the opportunity to learn the track, and the circuit people the chance to organize themselves, before we get down to the regular schedule of practice and qualifying sessions on the Friday.

Assuming it is not a new venue, the drivers and the majority of the team personnel would tend to arrive at the circuit around lunchtime on the Thursday. At that stage the atmosphere is fairly relaxed, the pace seemingly quite leisurely, but the first-time observer can still get an indication of the scale of modern Formula One. It is a massive operation. Williams have a team of up to thirty-five people at the races; Renault are there with their own truck and ten people assigned to our job; Elf set up a field laboratory at each circuit. There are sixteen teams, all with their trucks lined up at the back of the pits, the other engine and fuel suppliers, plus the Goodyear corner of the paddock, with all the vehicles and equipment they require to serve the needs of the pit lane.

Grand Prix motor racing has come a long way since the days of the amateur enthusiasts. It is thoroughly professional and superbly organized. Credit for that goes to FISA, the governing body of world motor sport, and FOCA, the representative association of the constructors. FISA are responsible for the sporting and political side of Formula One, the regulations and safety. The medical operation at each circuit is headed by Prof. Sid Watkins, of the Royal London Hospital. He has a medical centre, a team of doctors and nurses, plus emergency cars, ambulances and, always

Above left Max Mosley, elected President of FISA in 1991

Above right Bernie Ecclestone, President of FOCA and Vice-President (Marketing) of FISA

on standby for more serious cases, a helicopter. There are also fire appliances at the ready.

In the autumn of 1991 we had a change at FISA, when Max Mosley, an Englishman, beat Jean-Marie Balestre, a Frenchman, in the presidential election. I, as I think most people, have mixed feelings about Balestre. He could be a strange man and a puzzle at times; one minute he'd be the most humane, caring, sensitive person in the paddock, the next quite the opposite. I have no doubt he is a genuine, sincere racing enthusiast who loves the sport, but he made some very harsh judgments. It was under his regime that, for example, I was black-flagged at Estoril in 1989 and then banned from the Spanish race which followed. That penalty had never been inflicted before and most observers agreed it was totally unreasonable, totally unjust. It was one of the worst episodes of my career, but I try not to bear grudges and, overall, I got on fairly well with him. He was a source of some fun and, although he occasionally criticized drivers in pre-race briefings, the drivers more than got their own back by teasing him unmercifully. Max Mosley has a very different personality and a very different approach, and I hope he will have a good, calming influence within the sport as a whole.

The man who has really made Formula One the great show and commercial success we have come to expect is Bernie Ecclestone, president of FOCA and now vice-president of FISA. He was responsible for getting the teams to make the commitment to go to all the races and thereby guarantee a package for the circuit organizers and television. What he has done for Formula One, and every one of us involved in Formula One, is quite phenomenal. He sets standards that anyone in business would be proud of. The record and stature of Formula One now speaks for itself: the

Paddock Club, Circuit of Catalonia, Spain 1992

viewing figures, the amenities, everything. He has the capacity to think of everything and has a great eye for detail. As far as I'm concerned, Formula One is what it is today largely because of Bernie.

The commercial development is apparent all about you at a Grand Prix weekend: the hospitality units, the relatively new F1 Paddock Club, where corporate sponsors can entertain their guests, plus, of course, the array of circuit advertising hoardings. In the Formula One paddock itself, the trucks and motorhomes bear the names and logos of team sponsors. It is a colourful, busy scene, which becomes even more colourful and considerably busier as the weekend progresses and the countdown to the Grand Prix itself gathers pace.

The paddock is like a village, and every other week of the summer the village appears at different circuits, in different countries of the world, but always looking much the same. You see the same transporters, the same motorhomes, the same faces: we're all here to put on a show. Some people may say it is an expensive sport to support and watch, and certainly it is not cheap, but I would argue very strenuously that it gives value for money. You must take into account that it is an extremely expensive sport to stage and a lot of other major sports probably wouldn't cost a hundredth of the price. The result is, I believe, a fabulous spectacle full of drama, excitement, and, very often, surprises.

Although, as I've said, the Thursday scene appears generally relaxed, the teams are soon into a tried and tested routine of preliminaries. I make sure I have a briefing with Patrick and my engineer, David Brown; there may be particular differences in the aerodynamics for the circuit, so that aspect is discussed with Adrian; often the tyre technicians come into the meeting. The object of the exercise is to try to anticipate and, if we sense there may

Clearing the view. Drivers often wear several layers of visors, to allow a dirty one to be stripped off during a race.

Opposite Working in the pits for Nigel's first race back with Williams, Phoenix, 1991

be a problem with the car, try to cure it. We are straight down to business; once a race weekend has begun, time is more crucial than ever. It is a race against time, just as it is a race against the fastest lap and beating the clock is what wins motor races.

Most of the circuits are established Grand Prix venues, so we will have data from previous races and, in many cases, from more recent testing to help us determine the settings for the cars, which by now will be taking familiar shape in the garage. We, in common with most teams, would normally take three cars to a race, though we carry enough parts virtually to rebuild a car if that becomes necessary. Riccardo and I have a car each, and there is a spare. I have first call on the spare, so that normally carries my red No. 5, but if Riccardo has to use it the lads whip off the 5 and stick on his white No. 6.

There are three mechanics on each of the three cars and each driver has his own engineer. My engineer, David, also oversees work on the spare car. David, my mechanics – Carl, Stuart and Gary – and I, are like a team within a team. They have to believe in the driver, as I certainly believe in them, my life is in their hands and I trust them with it. Unless you have that trust, that belief and that bond, you can't work as an effective unit. I like to think we have demonstrated just how well and how effectively we work together.

Each mechanic is responsible for a particular section of the car. Carl has the back; he's the gearbox man. Gary has the centre and takes charge of the suspension. Stuart, who takes the front, is the aerodynamics man. The intention is to get through the work as smoothly and efficiently as possible, without people falling all over themselves. It's a practical deployment.

Having said that, all the mechanics are capable of switching jobs or overlapping if there's a problem in a certain area. There's a great spirit and understanding between them and they work exceedingly well together.

It's incredible how well mechanics manage to get through their work considering the chaos in and around the pits at some races. As one of the top teams we are always the focus of a lot of attention from the media, sponsors, guests and the public. While we acknowledge the high profile nature of our sport and the commercial importance of exposure, no-one should lose sight of the fact that the pits and the pit lane area are, potentially, highly dangerous areas and congestion makes them even more so.

David oversees the whole programme on my car. He will ensure the flow of communications, with Peter Windsor, Adrian, Patrick and Frank. If technical decisions have to be made, Patrick comes in; if pressure has to be

Top left Being strapped in for action

Above left Monitoring the times of the opposition

Above Into the pit lane

exerted on any of our suppliers, because things are not up to standard or on schedule, that's Frank's department. He is the only one who can handle that and he handles it extremely well.

While the mechanics are working on the cars, the engineers are consulting and the tyre men are sorting out our supply with Goodyear. I will get through around twenty sets of tyres over the weekend. Our partners from Renault are organizing themselves, too. They bring to each race seven engines. Another three are sent to Williams in advance and those three are in the cars. Two new engines are kept back for the race. After the race, all ten engines are returned to Renault's factory to be stripped and examined. Renault technicians set up their banks of computers in a corner of our garage. Here, they can monitor the performance of the engines out on the circuit through telemetry equipment. The information is transmitted from the car to appear in graph-like form on a screen and allows them to trace the engine's performance on every corner and every straight of every lap. It is yet another measure of the technology in racing today.

After all the briefings are over, if we've satisfied ourselves everything is fine and there's enough time left in the day, I might play a few holes of golf. A number of the drivers are keen on golf and find it a good way to relax before getting down to the serious business of practice. I prefer to get back to the hotel and eat at a reasonable hour as I don't like eating too late. I normally eat pasta and salads, deliberately keeping off red meat this close to a race; pasta is good for energy and stamina. Eating sensibly and at sensible times is crucial. I am in bed by ten, or at the latest eleven, and with luck get a good night's sleep.

The boys, too, can usually get away from the circuit by around seven o'clock on the Thursday evening and they thoroughly deserve any chance they get for part of an evening off. They put in some incredibly long hours, sometimes even working through the night. It may seem a glamorous life, travelling the world as a mechanic with a top Grand Prix team. They must enjoy it because, otherwise, they wouldn't do it, but it is hard graft and, a lot of the time, anything but glamorous. Once you are inside a garage it doesn't really matter what country you are in.

On Friday morning the mechanics leave the hotel at around 6.45 to be at the track by 7.15 and begin the long, laborious procedure of warming up the cars. Right along the pits, you'll hear the rumbling of engines. The boys will snatch a quick breakfast and then be back in the garage between 8.00 and 8.15 to get on with the final phase of preparations before first practice, which starts at ten o'clock.

For the drivers reveille is usually about seven o'clock for eight o'clock at the circuit. I have breakfast there, but nothing heavy, perhaps some cereal or carrots and cheese, which I'm told are good for me. A thorough briefing follows, a recap of what we discussed the previous day and a revision if conditions have changed to the extent that we feel it's desirable. Weather and track can change overnight, and in Formula One, anything can so it's important to make sure everyone is fully aware of, and happy with, the game plan. If that is the case, then we can have a relatively quiet morning getting the job done.

The ideal scenario is to have a trouble-free weekend and be fastest in every session, getting the car going as quickly and reliably as possible and posting the times. That sounds very easy, but in reality, of course, it is not. Everyone else is trying to do the same and many are going to be very competitive. What's more, problems may crop up which will throw your programme into disarray. In the middle of the 1991 season we actually had a couple of perfect race weekends, back-to-back: at the British Grand Prix, and again at the German, a fortnight later, I was quickest in all the practice and qualifying sessions, and also won the races. Everything went just about like clockwork; we got through the work, we had the reliability and we had the speed. Unfortunately, spells like that are rare, yet it does show it can be done and the example serves as an incentive.

Sometimes you have to be prepared to forfeit the prospect of fastest time in any given practice session to find the right set-up of the car for the race. In 1989 I actually did that in qualifying for the Hungarian Grand Prix, on a circuit where overtaking is very difficult. I lined up for the race 12th on the grid, but I'd made sure the car was right and I won the race.

On the Friday and Saturday we have practice sessions morning and afternoon. The first session, which runs from ten to 11.30, is known as

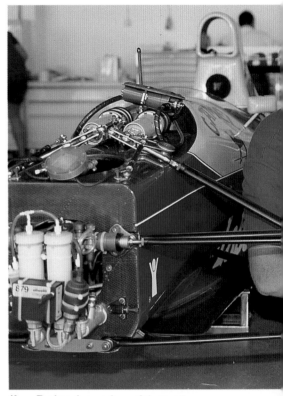

Above Brakes demand careful attention

untimed or free, or unofficial practice. Rather confusingly, perhaps, for anyone new to Formula One, since this session is timed, but the lap times do not affect the make-up of the starting grid for the race. Positions on the grid are determined by the times in timed or official practice, more usually referred to as qualifying. This is the second session on Friday and Saturday, held between one o'clock and two o'clock.

Before first practice the boys will push the car up to the circuit scales to weigh it and make sure it is not under the limit. We know already from our own scales that it is all right, but scales can vary a little from place to place, so we always take the precaution of checking. It is another example of the detailed planning teams go into. The cars will be checked by officials during the course of practice to make sure they comply with regulations. They are weighed with the drivers in the cockpit, which is why we are all weighed at the start of the season and again half way through, as the weight of the driver is subtracted to arrive at the weight of the car.

When the car is back in the garage, the mechanics will make a series of final checks, just contenting themselves – and the driver – that all is well. A mechanic might give the bodywork a quick clean because any resistance can affect the performance to some degree, but every team also prides itself on turn-out.

Some drivers sit around, chatting or whatever, until ten o'clock, but I tend to prefer to get on with it as soon as possible. I'll get into the car well ahead of the start time and make my way down to the end of the pit lane, ready to be out on the circuit the moment the red light turns to green. Occasionally the start is delayed, perhaps because one of the emergency

Below Winning for Ferrari at the 1989 Hungarian Grand Prix from 12th place on the grid

crews is not in position, or a section of the track needs sweeping, or the power is down. Hold-ups also occur once the session has started, perhaps because a car has hit a barrier and repairs are needed, or because of oil on the circuit. Whatever the reason, the clock is stopped temporarily and we always complete a full hour and a half. Qualifying will be put back to start an hour and a half after the end of untimed practice and will run for an hour, excluding time for any stoppages.

For most of the morning session we concentrate on achieving the optimum balance for the Grand Prix itself. We'll run on full tanks and try to set up the car in such a way that it can be driven positively in slow, medium and fast gear corners. A driver wants to be able to attack the corners and feel he cannot take them any quicker, so both the aerodynamic package and the engine must be right. Often a compromise is necessary, in that you may use more wing to get improved grip through the corners at the expense of straight-line speed. The aim is to come up with the best overall package, and the gauge for that is the clock.

Timing, like just about everything else in Formula One, is highly sophisticated. Long gone are the days of the stop-watch and clipboard, certainly as far as the official time-keeping is concerned, although team members may keep their own check on progress, and the pit-board is still used as a method of communication between team and driver. Formula One has an excellent timing service, previously provided by Olivetti-Longines and now courtesy of Olivetti and their new partners TAG-Heuer. Beams and individual sensors register a car's lap time instantly, to a thousandth of a second. Officials, teams and the media are able to follow developments as the times flash up onto their screens. Even during 'untimed' practice, this is an invaluable service as a team can compare its own performance with that of its rivals. At the end of each session a print-out of every lap time recorded by every car is available together with speed checks at a couple of key points on the circuit. All this information helps build up an overall picture of events on the circuit during any given practice session or, indeed, race.

It had become the custom to use the closing stages of morning practice to try the car on qualifying tyres in readiness for the afternoon session. However, Pirelli's withdrawal from Grand Prix racing left Goodyear as the sole supplier of tyres for 1992, and it was decided that, on the grounds of cost, they could not justify the production of 'qualifying' tyres. These tyres were made from very much softer compound than race tyres, to generate heat quickly, give greater grip and therefore yield faster times. They also, inevitably, wore out very quickly, normally giving just one flying lap. With only two sets of tyres available to each driver in the qualifying session, there were only two real chances of producing a good time.

These regulations made for a dramatic session. The possible perils of qualifying, with cars going flat-out in short bursts, are obvious, but at least with qualifying tyres there was a natural limitation on the number of cars out on the track at any given time. With race tyres, there can be thirty cars on the circuit for an hour, doing as many laps as they wish. This must make qualifying more dangerous which is why I hoped qualifying tyres would stay. My fears were confirmed in qualifying for the 1992 Mexican Grand Prix, where several drivers, including Senna, went off. Mistakes are inevitable when drivers are pushing themselves for many laps, trying to protect or improve grid positions. On a circuit as bumpy as Mexico, those mistakes can be costly, but thankfully no-one was seriously hurt. With or without qualifying tyres, the car also has to be tried on near empty tanks, so that by

Most meals are eaten in the motorhome and are provided by 'motorhomers' Peter and Jane Gurr.

the end of the morning session, all homework is satisfactorily completed. If a team finishes the morning declaring themselves 'in good shape', you'll know they've done that.

There is, though, no time to stop, no time to be smug. Formula One has a way of bringing you back down to earth with a bump the moment you think you've ironed out all the problems. Practice is followed by de-briefing. Analysis has to be very concise: on what happened, when, and what part of the car has contributed to making it quicker or slower. That catalogue is vitally important. A mistake at this stage can steer the programme in the wrong direction. The mechanics, meanwhile, are draining the cars and assessing what work has to be done before qualifying.

I may have a light lunch of fruit or some plain pasta, or plain bread with some fluids, or maybe not. I have no hard and fast rules and it largely depends on whether or not I'm hungry. I certainly don't want to eat too much as I'll soon be back in the car and out on the track again for the first qualifying session.

You pump yourself up for qualifying, although the judgement of when to go out is not so critical with race tyres, for the reasons we've covered. But it is still a matter of trying to work out when the traffic might be lighter and therefore give you a chance of going for a really quick lap. Grid positions, remember, are at stake here. The two sets of tyres consigned to each driver are marked and checked by officials before the car is allowed to leave the pit-lane for the circuit. Once out there, you require a little luck and a lot of co-operation from the other drivers, especially when overtaking. If you get that co-operation, and the faster cars get a fair opportunity, this one-hour session can be great entertainment. It is almost a contest in its own right. There may be another qualifying session to come, but you need the insurance of a good time on the first day, in case it should rain on the second day and make it impossible to improve.

It can be very frustrating – as well as dangerous – if you are balked on a really fast lap. All too often, some drivers don't appear to use their mirrors. You can also be angry with yourself if you feel you haven't got it exactly right or pushed hard enough at a certain corner. You are striving for the perfect lap because it usually takes something close to perfection to get pole position. That is the standard you have to set yourself at the very top.

At the end of the first qualifying session we have a provisional grid of twenty-six cars, arranged in order according to their times. All of these, plus the four who haven't made the overnight starting list, will get a second chance on Saturday afternoon, but emotions and reactions still reflect the varying fortunes. There are tales of woe and tales of optimism. Up and down the pit lane, the inquests have begun. The length of de-briefing, usually held in a section of the transporter, is also likely to reflect fortunes in the session. If everything has worked out well, it can be short, yet it can also be very long. Ideally, it should be very businesslike: identifying any problems, coming up with a solution and then acting on it. Of course views sometimes differ, so you try to reach the right verdict as quickly as possible. You are fighting against time and you become ever-more conscious of that the deeper you get into the weekend.

The lads get on with one or two routine jobs at the end of the session and actually have lunch at about 2.20. We are all watered and fed by our 'motorhomers', Peter and Jane Gurr, two very important members of the team. Within twenty minutes the mechanics are back at work in the garage. They will have a job list from the race engineer and have to get on with it. That list, and the time it takes to work through it, depends on the performance during the day, whether there are to be any major changes to the car and whether there have been any mechanical problems. If an engine change is required it will mean a stint of hard work, down on their knees for something like three hours. If they are lucky, they could be finished at about 7.30 on Friday night. If they are not lucky, it could be any time before they are through.

The driver, too, could be in for a long afternoon and evening, even though his driving duties are over. Williams has a number of major sponsors, and part of the job involves appearing at their functions and meeting their guests. At some races the schedule of commitments and engagements is quite considerable. Apart from appearances for sponsors there are always requests for television, radio and Press interviews. On top of all that there are the demands of the fans for autographs and so on. There is very little time left for family and friends, who may be accompanying you. It can be hectic, but I accept that this is part and parcel of the job in Formula One and I like to think I give as much time to this side of it as any driver. I have already tried to explain what the fans mean to me. One year at Monza, well into Saturday evening, I started signing autographs and before too long I was standing on the pit wall, conducting the fans' singing and chanting. Moments such as that are very precious and stay with you forever.

If I have an engagement on the Friday evening, I'll still try to get back to my hotel at a respectable hour for a good night's sleep before a second day of practice. Saturday is basically a carbon copy of Friday in terms of the time-table and the routine. The significant difference, of course, is that we are that much closer to the race and the completion of preparations. This

BBC's Murray Walker is put in the picture, South Africa, 1992

is the last full day of practice and the last full day in which to get it right. You become very conscious that any mistake now, any time lost now, could prove very costly. Concentration and application are vital.

The work done that Saturday morning, in free practice, will give you the parameters for the race. This is when you need to put in the mileage and be absolutely certain you've got the car right in race condition. It is also important to run the spare car and make sure you are happy with that, because if there's a last minute hitch with the regular race car, you may have to switch. Most drivers are reluctant to do that because, although the cars are identical, you always get a certain 'feel' for your race car. It may be psychological to some extent, but you just feel happier. Having said that, I have won with the spare car and there should be no question of it being inferior.

Another 'de-brief' follows morning practice and then, almost before you have had time to think, the final qualifying session is upon you. Usually the times on Saturday are better than those on the Friday. The track will, by now, be cleaner and have more rubber down because of the traffic it has had running on it, which in turn means better grip and improved speeds.

The other ingredient which can bring down the times in the second qualifying session is the competition. The tension and drama may be even greater than on the first day because pole position for the race really is the prize. That can mean more on some circuits than others. There are certain circuits where, because overtaking is all but impossible, if the cars are well matched, the man who gets pole and holds that advantage through the first

Lined up for the start of the 1992 season, at Kyalami (*left*) and Mexico, 1991 (*above*)

corner has virtually won the race. Even on the tracks where it is possible to pass, any advantage is welcome. If it rains on race day, the man at the front is the only one who can see. The rest are having to drive 'blind' through a wall of spray.

Apart from all the practical advantages of being on pole, just achieving it is a boost in itself. One of my most memorable poles came in the 1991 British Grand Prix at a newly-rebuilt Silverstone. Into the closing stages of the session I was quickest, but Senna still had his second set of tyres available to him, as I had. The onus was on him to attack my time, and I hoped he wouldn't be able to beat it, but to be perfectly honest I thought he would. So, as he went round, I sat in my car. It's important not to relax too much but to keep yourself in a state of readiness. Sure enough, Ayrton went faster, and his name appeared at the top of the screen in front of me. I nodded to my team, 'Let's go.' I wanted that pole back, especially here, at my home Grand Prix. There really is something about my home race that enables me to find that bit extra, and that Saturday afternoon, I was able to find a very special lap. I beat Senna's time by seven-tenths of a second and had pole. It was a fabulous moment and the response from the crowd made it better still.

The weekend goes on, though, and soon you have to turn your attention to the race, even after a qualifying session such as that. De-briefing will point the way for the absolutely vital work carried out on Saturday evening. Now the car is being set up for the warm-up the following morning, prior to the actual race. You will be running on full tanks and in race trim. Everything is checked and double checked in the minutest detail to make

sure every part of the aerodynamic package is right.

If I have managed to get away from the circuit in the afternoon to have a bath and change, and don't have any work to do for sponsors, I will come back to the circuit most Saturday nights to try to give the mechanics a bit of moral support. They always work late the night before the race. There's an engine change and a thousand other things to be done, so they probably won't get to bed until the early hours – and they still have to be back on parade first thing in the morning. It was four o'clock when the last of them left the circuit on the morning of the 1992 South African Grand Prix.

I may watch television for a while before turning in, mainly to relax and unwind. The race doesn't prey on my mind but I can hardly dismiss it! I might make a mental plan of my start or the race overall. There may be an important decision to be made regarding tyres: there are slight variations of race tyre compounds, and the choice could depend on the track surface or race strategy – whether we wish to use a harder compound and not stop for a change, or opt for the softer compound and make a pit stop.

The final decisions will be taken after warm-up, which starts four-and-a-half hours before the race, and lasts for only half an hour. This, rather than qualifying, should provide a fairly accurate guide to what is likely to happen in the Grand Prix itself. There may be a little 'kidology' here and there with cars on half empty tanks, but most of the teams are having a serious last run with a full fuel load and genuine race trim. There's time for only half a dozen or so laps, so you want no mistakes. If you haven't got it right now, you really do have problems. Having said that, there is always the exception that proves the rule. At my first race for Ferrari, the 1989 Brazilian Grand Prix, we had so much trouble in warm-up I didn't complete a proper lap. Nobody expected me to last ten laps of the race and I booked an early flight home. What happened? The car just kept running, I kept over-taking people and won.

Such instances are sweet yet rare. The last thing you want between warm-up and race is a desperate scramble. The four-hour gap gives teams the

Below Taking one of Monaco's famous corners in 1991

time for unscheduled work, even an engine change, but ideally you want to use it methodically putting the final touches to the weekend operation. People rushing around in a panic increase the risk of a silly slip-up which could prove very expensive by the end of the afternoon.

An hour after warm-up, drivers and team managers are summoned to an official briefing, which is no longer the major production Jean-Marie Balestre tended to turn it into. Max Mosley made an appearance after he was elected president and told us he did not intend to do so in future. He was content to leave it to his officers to run through any points of procedure deemed necessary. Often, following the drivers' briefing, I will have a sponsor's presentation to attend. I may talk the guests round the circuit, indicating on a map the gear changes and speeds. It's fascinating to see people's reactions when they get close to it for the first time as it's only now that they begin to grasp the speeds, and the amazing acceleration and deceleration of Formula One cars. No matter how good and impressive it is on television, you have to see it live to appreciate the spectacle fully.

It is a day-long show, with support races, maybe an air display and other demonstrations. The stands will have been full from early morning, creating a colourful backdrop and tremendous atmosphere. I naturally find Silverstone very stimulating, but there are many other fabulous racing scenes. The Italian crowds make Monza and Imola very special, Monaco is unique because of its tradition and prestige and Adelaide has become one of the great favourites with everyone in Formula One.

For lunch on race day I'll have a little pasta, no more. The important thing is to take in as much fluid as possible because in certain hot and demanding conditions, a driver can lose anything up to seven pounds. After lunch I try to rest for half-an-hour to an hour in the motorhome. I may not necessarily sleep, but any rest is worthwhile.

The team will have taken the opportunity over the course of the weekend to practise pit stops, which can literally win or lose races for a driver as our unfortunate experience at Estoril, in 1991, demonstrated. Things can go wrong, so you keep working at it to make sure you not only do it quickly – ideally inside eight seconds – but also do it right. We invested in new equipment and spent considerable time practising the pit-stop routine before the 1992 season. The man with the 'lollipop' controls the operation, guiding the driver in and holding him with a 'brakes on' reminder. As the car is jacked up, three mechanics go to work on each wheel. One goes in with the air gun and takes out the wheel nut, the second removes the wheel, the third replaces it, and the gun man moves in again to tighten it. When all four gun men indicate they are clear, the jacks go down and the lollipop man releases the car. Other members of the team may, meanwhile, have been cleaning the driver's visor, or clearing any waste paper from the radiators. There will also be someone on hand with a fire extinguisher. Fuel stops were banned a few years ago on safety grounds, and fire precautions in the garage area are constantly being revised.

Over the course of the weekend security teams also keep watch on the garages. There have been suspicions of espionage, and Elf once discovered a sample of their fuel had been stolen. We have also had an instance of sabotage in a team's garage. Security, therefore, needs to be tight.

Three-quarters-of-an-hour before the race, however, the last thing on a driver's mind is security. He's in the garage, making personal, final preparations. I'm already wearing my fire-proof race-suit and I may be fixing a visor on my helmet. Drivers often fix a number of visors, which they can tear off during the course of the race as they get dirty. I regard my

Above A flame-proof balaclava is worn underneath the helmet

Above right Helmet and gloves complete the kit

helmet as sacrosanct and don't like anybody touching it. If I felt someone had been tampering with it, I'd never wear it again. A helmet is a very personal piece of equipment; it can save your life.

Beneath the helmet we wear a protective balaclava, and I also have a neck-brace, which I've used since I broke my neck in 1977. On come the gloves and it's into the car, sliding down the narrow cockpit. I have a drink supply pipe and an emergency oxygen supply line. There is also a small fire extinguisher in the car. I have radio contact with the team, though that cannot always compete with the noise of the engine. I prefer to use it just when I have to, but I'm told I sometimes talk quite a lot!

The pressure going into the race very much depends on whether you feel you're the underdog or that you should win. The pressure is greater if you feel you should win and this is where experience is invaluable. You know how to cope with the situation, just as you've coped with the entire weekend and the longer you do it, the better you get at it. I know how far I can push myself, both on and off the circuit.

Half-an-hour before the start of the race, the exit from the pit lane is opened. In fifteen minutes it will be closed again, and anyone not out on the circuit by then will have to start from the pit lane. Most cars will go round the circuit a couple of times, making sure all is well, before taking their places on the staggered grid. What I do in those last few minutes varies from circuit to circuit, climate to climate. If it's cold and windy I'll stay in the car, if it's very hot I may sit outside the car, under an umbrella, drinking water. I may want to pop to the bathroom; I may chat to people I know.

When I'm strapped in the car again, waiting for the signal to start the formation lap, I occasionally have my worries. It depends on the cir-

The vital pit stop at the 1992 Brazilian Grand Prix

Left Off-duty with friend Robin Oake, Isle of Man Chief Constable, at the 1992 South African Grand Prix

Above Mark McNulty, outstanding pro' golfer and close friend, with Nigel in the motorhome at Silverstone, June test 1992.

Below Poised for the off

cumstances and the importance of the race. It's not so much from the safety aspect but because I'm hoping nothing goes wrong with the car and that I make a good start. If you are on pole position or second place, you're looking to get into the lead straight away. If you're in third or fourth place, you're thinking you might – depending on the circuit – be able to make up a couple of places from the start. At the very least, you want to get away well enough to prevent anyone passing you and to give yourself the best possible position coming out of the first corner. But no matter what your calculations, anything can happen when you come round to the grid and slowly line up for the real thing. Soon the red light is on, then the green, the adrenalin in every driver pumping. We are away in an explosion of noise. All the weekend's effort has built up to this, the Grand Prix. The teams can do very little now but watch and wait: it's down to the car and the driver.

I hope I won't have any problems, in which case I shan't see them again until the end of the race. Better still, I'll be the driver taking the chequered flag and standing at the top of the podium. That is a magical moment which can never lose its appeal and is a moment for all the team to savour. The

Fleet Street scribes get the Mansell
verdict, South Africa, 1992

driver does the round of television and Press interviews, but every member of the team has earned the success, and the satisfaction is justly shared by all.

Then, almost before you have a chance to take it in, the celebrations and the race weekend are over. The crowds have gone, the motorhome people are pulling down their awnings, the teams are packing their trucks. For our boys it's another long job, perhaps four hours, loading everything up. Back at the factory, they'll have to strip down the cars and begin the process all over again. In a fortnight there will be another show, another race weekend.

The Races

*F*ormula One is truly the motor racing championship of the world. It circles the globe from Johannesburg to Japan, from the Americas to Australia, taking in many European countries en route. The sixteen races are held in vastly contrasting settings, on circuits of distinctly varying design, speeds and demands, testing the versatility and consistency of man and machine.

The United States was an unfortunate loss to the 1992 calendar, even if it hasn't proved winning territory for me. Formula One had problems getting a foothold in a country with such obvious potential and stature, largely because the Americans have their own form of racing, just as they have their own form of football, and a mania for baseball. I would like to think, though, that the US will play a part in Formula One's future. If it did, it would certainly serve further to enhance the credibility of the sport.

Having said that, political changes allowed us to return to South Africa for the start of the '92 season, so another continent has been added to the tour. For me it meant something of a sentimental journey because I had won the last race there in 1985, even though it is hardly the same track. The Kyalami circuit, near Johannesburg, has been re-built and the lay-out and facilities brought into line with the modern requirements of the authorities. It can be very hot at Kyalami and that, added to altitude, makes it a potentially very demanding venue both for the driver and the engine. The air may be rather cleaner than it is in Mexico, but you can still find yourself gasping for breath. Acclimatization is therefore particularly important, and I headed for Kyalami a week ahead of the '92 race. What's more, I wanted to make sure I was up to speed right from the start of the season. I was very conscious of the need to give myself the best possible chance out of the blocks, so my physical and mental state had to be right.

That 1985 win was the second of my Formula One career, coming immediately after my maiden victory in the Grand Prix of Europe at Brands Hatch. It was satisfying to be able to show, straight away, that Brands was no one-off. The experience of winning and the confidence that generated fortified me, and I was on pole for Kyalami. The race came down to a great

Formula One's farewell appearance at
Phoenix, 1991

Overleaf The re-built Kyalami Circuit,
1992

Above Then, as now, a winner as at the 1985 South African Grand Prix

Opposite Fighting for position at the start of the 1992 South African Grand Prix

Left Still King of Kyalami, 1992

scrap between me and my Williams team-mate, Keke Rosberg. I made it home first, and Keke completed an outstanding one-two for the team. Encouragingly, I was first, ahead of Riccardo, to give Williams another maximum score at the 1992 South African Grand Prix. I led every practice and qualifying session, and, although I switched to my spare car for the race, because of concerns about an electrical problem, I opened my campaign with the victory I wanted. Senna was third in the McLaren.

I have also won in Mexico, and had second places there, but I have very mixed feelings about the place. Mexico City sprawls endlessly, with a population of something like eighteen million. As well as the altitude, there is the infamous smog to cope with and it is advisable to go well stocked with throat sweets. It also pays to be extremely careful what you eat and drink. I am not the only driver who has been a victim of Montezuma's revenge! My uncomfortable experience was in 1986, and life wasn't much better in the race. I couldn't find first gear on the startline, crawled away in second with most of the other cars in front of me, and had to settle for fifth place.

Mexico never gives a smooth ride. The circuit is built on a lake bed, so it is hardly surprising the road surface is not level. Some parts are terribly bumpy – and dangerous. After the 1991 race weekend – when Ayrton Senna was one of several drivers who went off – the local authorities promised to consider modifications to the Peralta Curve, an incredible right-hander, taken flat-out at speeds up to 180 mph. The bumps and lack of run-off area made it one of the most dangerous corners in the world. The track is also very dirty, which means it can be difficult to get good grip. In 1992, however, conditions were if anything even worse. Senna again had an accident in qualifying, badly bruising his left leg. Setting up the car is a compromise here and no easy task.

The Mexico City circuit (called the Autodromo Hermanos Rodriguez) does at least have a spacious pit lane and pits area, and the track has produced some fabulous racing since it was put back on the Formula One map in 1986. The Peralta leads onto a long straight, where there is plenty of opportunity for overtaking, and there are other sections where passing is possible too. It is a very challenging circuit.

I won the '87 Mexican Grand Prix, which was run in two parts because of the hold-up after Derek Warwick went off. I had to retire there in '88 and '89, but the following year I was second after a terrific dice with Gerhard Berger. I was in a Ferrari, he was in a McLaren. The way he went past me upset me. He locked up on the inside and pushed me out of the way, so I went after him, determined to retrieve that second place. I decided to go for it at the Peralta – on the outside. I committed myself, flat, knowing that if I managed to get round I was bound to come out of the corner ahead of him – and that's exactly what I did. It was a great fight and Gerhard said he'd enjoyed it just as much as I had.

Top right Starting grid in Mexico, 1987

Bottom right Negotiating the modified Peralta Curve, 1992

Above On course for another Mexican victory, 1992

Back with Williams, I was second again in '91, finishing strongly but not quite able to make up the deficit on my partner, Riccardo Patrese. That one-two confirmed Williams' form and set us up for what was to be a tremendously productive middle part of the season. In 1992 I reversed the positions, as we strengthened our early championship lead. Ayrton was able to race but was forced to retire, and third place went to Michael Schumacher, in a Benetton Ford.

Another bitter-sweet Grand Prix for me is that in Brazil. The Interlagos circuit, at Sao Paulo, is an excellent venue; it was rebuilt and took over as the Championship track from Rio's Jacarepagua in 1990. It was imaginatively designed, making use of the rolling terrain, and provides a good test for the driver. This, though, is another city where you have to be careful what you eat and drink.

I won the last race at Rio (I seem to have a habit of closing down circuits!) on my first outing for Ferrari. It really was a 'dream debut' because, as I have already explained, we'd had so much trouble with the car that weekend we thought we'd be packing up and heading for home after a few laps. Instead, the car seemed to get stronger and stronger and, although I was convinced it was going to let me down, I made it to the line first. It was an amazing day.

Still with Ferrari, I was fourth at Interlagos in 1990 and saw the prospect of winning with Williams in '91. I started third on the grid and got away well, moving straight into second place, ahead of Riccardo and behind Senna. Although Ayrton opened a small gap I wasn't alarmed and began to close it. The gap opened up again, however, after I had a problem pulling away from a pit stop. I went back to work again only to be forced in for another change. It was discovered I had a gash in one of my tyres. Yet again

Opposite Michael Schumacher joins the champagne celebrations, Mexico, 1992

I set about catching the McLaren and was doing so at the rate of two or three seconds a lap, when, before I could launch a final attack, the gearbox gave up on me and I spun out of the race. Riccardo, coming up behind, wasn't able to stop Ayrton claiming his first win on home ground. The following year nothing could stop us. I was in pole for the third time, Riccardo second on the grid, but he had a much better start. I followed him until the pitstops, then found myself in the lead and managed to open a comfortable gap. I had three wins from three races; a dream start. We were reaping the rewards of all our hard work, yet felt McLaren, who had problems with their new car that weekend, were bound to come back. As it was, Schumacher gave Benetton another third place.

Barcelona, too, has an excellent new circuit, which has now taken over from Jerez as the stage for the Spanish Grand Prix. Both venues have served me well, but there is no doubt that Barcelona is head and shoulders above Jerez, which was narrow, twisty and offered little opportunity for overtaking. The crowds were also disappointingly small. Despite that, I can't complain about my races there. Formula One's first visit to Jerez was in 1986, when I made a lunge at Senna's Lotus on the finishing line only to be edged out by 0.014 seconds. The following season, I had my first Spanish success, giving myself a cushion in the early stages and completing the job quite comfortably. Ideally, you want to win a race at the slowest possible pace, doing no more than you have to.

In '88 I had no such luxury, having to work for all my worth in the normally-aspirated Judd-powered Williams to get close to Alain Prost's

Patrese's brilliant start in Brazil, 1992

Previous page The challenging Interlagos Circuit, 1991

Below 'Dream debut' for Ferrari, 1989

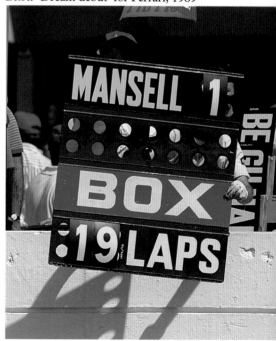

Victory over Senna on home ground,
1992

Barcelona is put on the Formula One map,
1991

McLaren Honda turbo. The power differential that season was a joke, the Honda always had plenty in hand, and I had to take second place again that day. I wasn't even in the event twelve months later, because I had been suspended for one race following the black flag fiasco at Estoril. In '90 I was back with another second place.

The Circuit of Catalonia, north-east of Barcelona, is an undulating track with a nice mix of corners and the all-important long straight, which ensures adequate opportunity for passing. The general lay-out of the circuit and the facilities, including an enormous media centre, made it, by common consent, a welcome addition to Formula One. For me, the 1991 Spanish Grand Prix was an incident-packed meeting from start to finish. At the end of it, my doctor wanted to know if I'd become a triathlete! On the Friday evening, following the first qualifying session, I played football for a team of Formula One journalists in their annual match against the photographers. There was a bit of needle here and there, but nothing serious, and I was thoroughly enjoying myself, getting rid of some more post-Estoril frustration. (This time it was the wheel-nut incident.) I hit two goals and, with the score at 2–2 nearing the end, ran through hoping to get the winner.

First leg of the triathlon, FOPA, the photographers' team *versus* the Camel press team, 1991

Highlight of the 1991 season, the duel with Senna

Their goalkeeper, the Italian driver, Fabrizio Barbazza, blocked my shot and as I pounced on to the rebound I went crashing to the ground with damaged tendons in my ankle. I was in agony and had ice packs on it most of the weekend. I don't think the team, my racing team, that is, were too amused.

I was determined not to let it affect my driving and qualified second on the grid, behind Gerhard and immediately ahead of Ayrton. By Sunday the pain was worse than ever and I hobbled into the drivers' briefing. I had to pass Gerhard to get to a row of empty seats and as I did so he aimed a playful kick at my swollen ankle. I winced and suggested to him that it wasn't a very intelligent thing to do, but he thought it was funny and kicked it again. I tried to hold his leg out of the way but he kicked me a third time. That was more than enough, so I replied with one swift and effective blow to the solar plexus and told him he was a fool if he thought it was funny, and sat down. It was all over in a matter of seconds and it's an incident we would both now prefer to forget. That, then, was the boxing leg of my triathlon. The serious part, the motor racing, was still to come. It also proved to be the best part.

A drizzle made slicks too much of a risk, especially as I was starting off-line, and I carefully picked my way round the first lap. Michael Schumacher went by, but there was no point in resisting at that stage. On the second lap I retrieved third place and chased Senna. I tracked him into the last corner

of the fourth lap, a sweeping right-hander, ready to attack on the straight. I pulled out from under his rear wing and up alongside. We stayed side by side, our wheels barely a couple of inches apart, hurtling down to the right turn at around 190 mph. There's no doubt it was a test of nerve and, I suppose, a matter of pride. Neither man wanted to give way and that one scene somehow captured the drama of the entire Championship contest between us.

I had the inside line approaching the corner and intended to keep it. We braked as late as possible and he didn't try anything silly. I went through ahead of him and, although he attempted to fight back, I stayed there. Many observers rated that duel as the highlight of the season.

Spectacular and breathtaking though it was, we were still only on the fifth lap, and changing conditions piled up the imponderables. A dry line was already appearing and soon we were diving into the pits for slicks. When we settled down again, I was back in third place and Senna was in the lead! Gerhard moved in front of his team-mate again and, as I closed up on Ayrton, he spun coming out of the last corner on lap thirteen and almost collected me because he selected reverse to come back onto the track. That scare over, I chased Gerhard. He knew what to expect on the straight and defended, yet I probably took him by surprise when I dived past on a much slower, downhill section. It was tight, but I made it and opened up a four-second gap. Gerhard eventually had to retire, leaving backmarkers as my only real concern. I came through unscathed and had my second Spanish victory. I had to win to retain any hope of winning the Championship, and I was determined I'd do just that. It was a great first Grand Prix for the

Opposite Start of the 1992 Spanish Grand Prix. It had been declared a 'wet race' before the start and Mansell successfully fended off Schumacher for another victory (*right*).

Above The *tifosi* massed on the huge banks at Imola and (*opposite below*) supporters at the 1992 San Marino Grand Prix

Opposite above Accelerating away to a record fifth consecutive victory at San Marino at the start of the 1992 season

Overleaf Monaco, the race that gets ever-harder

Barcelona circuit and it was generally acknowledged as the outstanding race of the season. We had to contend with increasingly wet conditions in the 1992 Spanish Grand Prix, and even drivers as good and experienced as Ayrton and Riccardo were caught out. Starting from pole, I had to fight off a fabulous sprint by Michael to equal Ayrton's record opening sequence of four wins the previous year. I was also very proud to have equalled the career total of twenty-five victories achieved by Jim Clark and Niki Lauda.

Imola hosts Italy's 'other' Formula One race, the San Marino Grand Prix. You will have gathered by now that I love the Italian fans, so it may not surprise you to learn this is one of my favourite venues. The crowds are marvellous. Inside, they pack the stands and hills, outside they erect scaffolding to get a view over the perimeter walls and fencing. They are truly passionate about their racing. The circuit, named after Enzo and Dino Ferrari, matches the atmosphere. It is very challenging and a difficult place to find the right set-up. It's also one of the few anti-clockwise tracks. It climbs and falls, has some very tricky corners and some extremely fast sections. None of us will ever forget that dreadful day in 1989 when Gerhard, then my team-mate at Ferrari, crashed, and his car burst into flames there. Mercifully, he came out of it with relatively minor burns, but we are all aware how lucky he was. I haven't always had much luck there in terms of results, though the 1987 race was a welcome exception. It wasn't one of my more flamboyant wins, but it was very satisfying in that it required good, sensible management. The track at Imola is notoriously 'thirsty', so it was a case of doing the job in the most conservative and economical way.

I was optimistic going into the 1991 Grand Prix, but my day wasn't to last long. At least I made the start that rainy day. Prost spun off on the parade lap, Berger did likewise yet managed to recover. I had problems right from the grid. I found myself in neutral instead of second, and Jean Alesi's Ferrari touched me as it went by on the grass. Before the end of the first lap I was hit again, this time by Martin Brundle's Brabham, and that was it. My race was over, and I was totally disgruntled. We were three races into the Championship and I hadn't a point or a finish to my name. Senna,

Opposite Monaco, shop window of
Formula One

meanwhile, collected win number three and had thirty points on the board.
In 1992 Imola marked my record fifth successive win.

Monaco is the most famous, glamorous and prestigious of all Grands
Prix, but I, like many of my colleagues these days, have a love-hate relationship with it. It is one of the greatest challenges of all, and no driver worth
his salt minds that. The trouble is that the Principality is so tiny and the
street circuit so tight, while Formula One has become enormous and
Formula One cars horrendously fast. It gets more difficult each year to race
on that track and to get the work done in the pits. This place, more than
any other, is where you have to marvel at the patience and diligence of the
teams; the pit lane is ludicrously narrow and outrageously over-crowded
with guests and hangers-on. We are all aware that this is THE shop-window
for the sport and that sponsors and their guests are very important, but
there really should be a more stringent control on numbers.

Out on the circuit it seems to get just as crowded. Overtaking is very
difficult because of the twists and turns. This is the slowest of all Grands
Prix, although it feels anything but slow when you are coming out of Casino
Square with the barrier leaping towards you. The camber here is just one
of the hazards and if you are not prepared it will catch you out. There are
so many worries here: debris, oil, sudden gusts of wind, the changing light
in and out of the tunnel. The track seems to get narrower every year. You
have to lean on the barriers to get the best possible time, knowing half an
inch too much can break the car. Precise judgement, as well as nerve, is
vital. When you've accomplished a good lap – and I have a healthy record

Below Start of the 1992 Monaco
Grand Prix

Opposite and right Snatching some time away from the circuit. With the family in Monaco and carp fishing in Montreal, 1992.

of front row positions here – you have a feeling of relief as much as elation. It is that sort of place.

In 1987 I had pole position and was comfortably ahead in the race, seemingly on the way to my first win at Monte Carlo. There was no need to lean on the barriers or even get remotely close to them. It really was that easy. Then, to my anguish, my exhaust broke and that was the end of my Monaco Grand Prix. My '88, '89 and '90 races brought only disappointment, too, but in '91 I managed the result which at last launched my Championship challenge.

For some time I feared it was going to be an all-too-familiar Monaco story for me because I had a problem with the engine's response. It was difficult to hold fourth place and eventually I had to give way to Prost. When Stefano Modena and Riccardo were forced out, Prost and I moved up to second and third places respectively. Gradually I got used to the response problem, which was caused by a fault in the throttle mechanism, and was able to pick up the pace. Coming out of the tunnel, fifteen laps from the end, I drew up on the Ferrari and dived inside as we plunged down the hill towards the chicane. Senna was well clear and there was nothing I could do about the McLaren, but I was more than satisfied with the outcome. A day of potential frustration had become a source of encouragement. I had second place and my first six points of the season. Senna, with forty, was still way ahead, yet he already sensed that he may not have been as secure as the drivers' Championship table indicated.

It is always a pleasure to go to Canada and the city of Montreal, and the Circuit Gilles Villeneuve, though rather bumpy in parts, is one most of the drivers find good to drive. It is situated on the Ile Notre Dame, an island in the St Lawrence, and provides a balanced test of ability. At each end is a hairpin, one of which is a popular overtaking point. There are flowing sections, where you try to find a rhythm, and a fast stretch spiced with awkward kinks.

All I had to show for my early races here was a broken wrist, the consequence of an accident in 1982, but my win in the 1986 Canadian Grand Prix made the wait and the pain worthwhile. It was one of those rare occasions when all the other leading drivers stayed the course, making the result even more satisfying. I ran the race at my pace, and took the flag ahead of Prost, Piquet, Rosberg and Senna. I was disqualified in the confusion at the start of the 1989 race, but that blow was nothing compared with the one awaiting me less than a mile from the end in 1991. I went in front of Riccardo at the first corner and led the race until the last lap. I was in total control, never under threat, and the car was fine. The win was mine – or so I believed. At the Pits Hairpin for the final time, the gearbox gave me neutral, and the engine cut out. The car just rolled to a halt. It was a most sickening experience, made all the more difficult to stomach by some ill-informed comments afterwards. The suggestion that I inadvertently flicked off the ignition is crazy. We had a computer 'glitch', and it shut down the system. Being classified sixth was scant consolation.

Apart from my own country, France has been one of my happiest hunting grounds in Formula One. I won at the Paul Ricard Circuit in 1986 and 1987, and was second there in 1989 after starting from the pit lane. In 1991, the race was taken from Provence to Burgundy, to a new track at Magny-Cours, near Nevers. The move, backed by Government money and influence, provided us with impressive facilities, a massive crowd, a beautifully smooth track but a lay-out which left much to be desired. Too many new generation circuits are being built with inherent problems, and

Above Start of the 1991 Canadian Grand Prix

Opposite Taking command at Montreal, 1991

Above Despair at the Pits Hairpin, 1991

Opposite Canada, 1991, the race that got away

this fell into that category. They tend to be too narrow, with too few places for over-taking and are therefore rather dull. The deficiencies were acknowledged by officials at Magny-Cours and modifications were promised. Circuit designers are rightly conscious of the safety standards required, but Barcelona has proved that you can make a new track which is both safe and challenging. It just requires a little imagination.

Even so, we had a great motor race at Magny-Cours in 1991 and it was certainly a fabulous day for me, for Williams and for our French engine partners, Renault. Ferrari's new car looked good that weekend, and the race soon became a contest between Prost and me. Alain was obviously keen to do well on home ground, and I was determined to register my first win of the season. Alain set the pace and I followed. I brought him within my range and seized my opportunity when we hit the traffic, darting through on the inside. Backmarkers are always liable to be a problem, one you have to address decisively. As it happened, Alain was given another chance by the tyre stops, which put him back in the lead, so I had to take up the chase again, and this time he was ready to cover the inside. What he clearly hadn't considered was a pass on the outside, and, as we came down towards the Adelaide hairpin on lap fifty-five, that is precisely what I pulled off. I went all the way round and through the right-hander with the lead. I was not about to give him a third chance.

It was my first victory since returning to the Williams fold and the seventeenth of my Formula One career, taking me past Stirling Moss's thirty-year-old English record. What's more, it elevated me to second place in the World Championship, above my team-mate, but still twenty-five points behind Senna. Next, though, was the British Grand Prix, at Silverstone, and twice before I had followed up French triumphs with success at the Northamptonshire circuit. We were apparently over our early season teething problems and there seemed no reason why I shouldn't complete an Anglo-French double.

Overleaf Start of the 1991 French Grand Prix

There is, as I have already said, something about racing on home ground

115

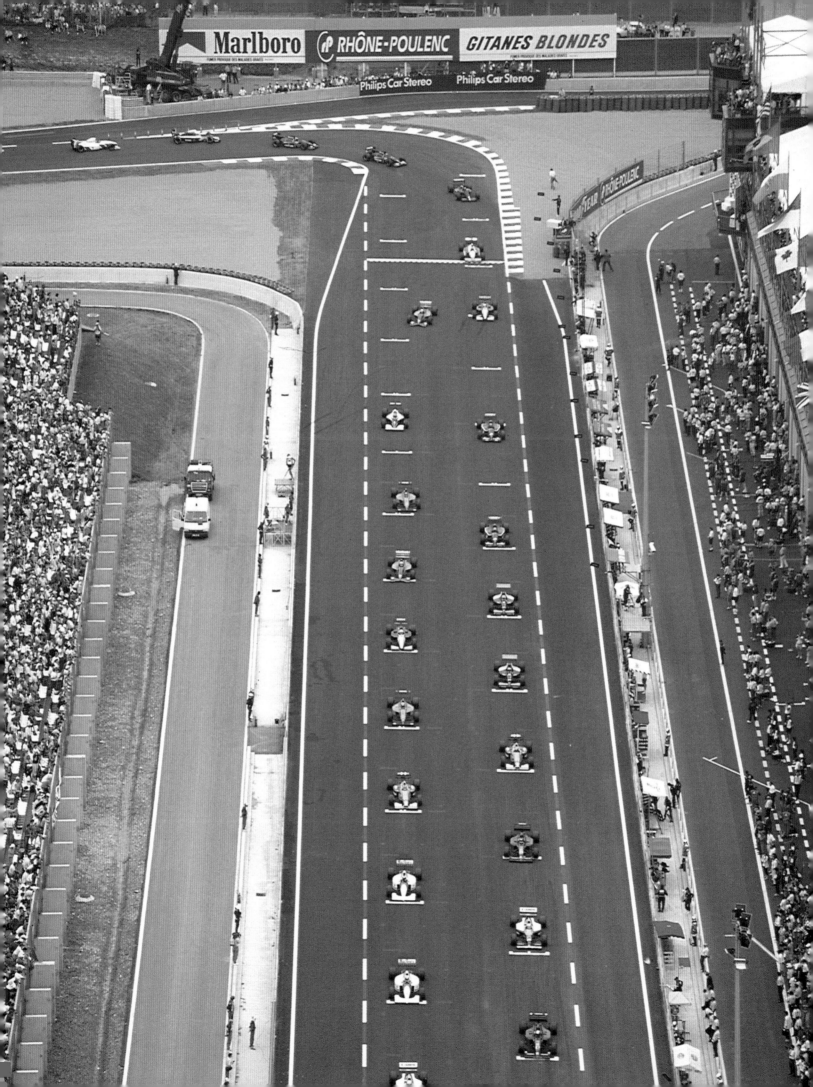

Opposite Magny-Cours, France's new
Grand Prix venue

On the grid at Magny-Cours before the start of the 1992 French Grand Prix. The race
was stopped and restarted because of poor weather conditions but Nigel won by a large
margin despite being twice beaten off the grid by Patrese. It was his sixth win of the season
and the twenty-seventh of his career, matching Jackie Stewart's record.

Maiden Formula One win, Brands Hatch 1985

which enables you to find that little extra within yourself, and I'm sure it's a feeling shared by other drivers. The whole occasion assumes added significance. Taking into account the 1985 Grand Prix of Europe, at Brands Hatch, my 1991 victory was the fourth in my own country. I had also had two second places, in 1988 and '89, and pole positions in '90 and '91.

That win at Brands was my first; very much the breakthrough. By the time we returned to the splendid Kent track, nine months later, for the British Grand Prix, I was not only used to winning races but mounting a challenge for the Championship. I won that 1986 race in the spare Williams, which had been set up by my then team-mate, Nelson Piquet. I was a little tentative in the early stages but gained confidence and had a tremendous battle with Nelson. When he missed a gear it was all I needed to go through. He chased back for a while but realized he couldn't break me and reluctantly accepted defeat.

Until that year, the British Grand Prix had alternated between Brands and Silverstone. Now, in line with FISA policy, each country has only one Grand Prix circuit and in Britain it is Silverstone, which was deemed to have greater potential for development. There is no question that the Silverstone authorities are exploiting that potential, expanding and improving the range of facilities and, in 1991, they rebuilt the circuit itself. Brands was a fantastic circuit, a driver's circuit and the natural amphitheatre made it a spectator's circuit too. It had character, but Formula One has now probably out-grown Brands, and the changes at Silverstone have turned it into a fantastic track for competitors and spectators alike.

Old friend, Greg Norman, joins the fan club at the 1987 British Grand Prix

Overleaf Silverstone, home of the British Grand Prix

For Silverstone weekend my family and I make our base the circuit infield. Together with a group of relatives and friends we set up camp in motorhomes and caravans. It's convenient, creates a nice atmosphere and we have a super time. A win makes it all the better, of course, and that was the outcome in 1987 after another fight with Nelson. I stopped to change wheels after losing a wheel balance and came out of the pits twenty-eight seconds down on him with thirty laps left. I began to eat into his advantage and realized I might catch him. The crowd sensed it too. They roared me round those closing laps and made sure I did catch him. I made a double feint down Hangar Straight and squeezed through at Stowe with a couple of laps to spare. At the end fans spilled onto the track, waving their Union Jacks. The scene was astonishing.

I had to settle for second place in 1988 and '89 but had only victory in mind after taking pole with the Ferrari the following year. The temperamental semi-automatic gearbox wouldn't co-operate, however, and I had to retire from the race. It was that evening I also announced my intention to retire from Formula One. It seemed the appropriate venue and would have been perfect from the top of the podium. That wasn't to be and, thanks to Frank, retirement wasn't to be, either.

In 1991, driving for Williams, we were back into the old routine. The difference was the circuit. Silverstone had been the fastest in the world. Keke Rosberg, at the wheel of a Williams Honda turbo, took pole for the 1985 British Grand Prix at a record average speed of 160.938 mph. Critics of Silverstone said it was flat, featureless and boring. It certainly wasn't

boring from the driving seat, not at those speeds, but the changes have definitely improved it. New corners and gradients have been introduced. It is no longer the fastest circuit (Monza now has that distinction) but I would say it is the hardest, the most gruelling in the world. It is more challenging for the drivers and has better viewing facilities for the public.

Senna hitches a lift back to the Silverstone pits

From my point of view the British Grand Prix is the hardest and most gruelling in terms of emotion and pressure, too. I get maximum aggravation and maximum satisfaction in that one weekend. The build-up starts probably a month in advance with demands for interviews and appearances. It grows during testing and reaches its climax at the race. Thankfully, the 1991 race was no anti-climax. It had been one of those rare weekends when just about everything had gone to plan. We took pole in that fabulous final qualifying session and the atmosphere was electric. There were probably 120,000 spectators there on race day and I couldn't help think something HAD to go wrong. In fact, the only slight hitch was at the start, when Ayrton got ahead of me, but I went for him as soon as possible, took him down Hangar Straight and led all the way from there.

What made it so extraordinary was the way the crowd maintained the noise level for the duration of the entire race. They were on their feet, cheering and waving, on every corner, on every lap. There was even a bonus for me. Ayrton ran out of petrol on the final lap, so I picked him up on my slowing-down lap and gave him a lift back to the pits. We both knew, though, that we wouldn't be exchanging many favours for the rest of the season. He led the Championship by eighteen points and I was determined to keep up the pressure.

I confess I didn't have such high hopes, though, for the German Grand Prix in 1991. Apart from a brief diversion to the new Nurburgring, Germany's venue for Formula One during my career has been Hockenheim, a

Above Home rule … fans at the 1991
British Grand Prix

Right 'One of those rare weekends when
just about everything had gone to plan'
Silverstone, 1991

Above The chequered flag marked the twenty-eighth win of Nigel's career, breaking Jackie Stewart's record

Opposite above Silverstone 1992. 150,000 jubilant fans swarmed onto the track after Nigel's spectacular victory, apparently oblivious to the cars still racing. Martin Brundle and Johnny Herbert also finished in the points.

Opposite below Nigel established a convincing lead early in the race and rewarded the crowd for their uproarious support with a new lap record in the closing laps of the race

Right A motorbike makes shuttling between pits and paddock easier

The lovely German town Heidelberg

circuit south-west of the lovely town of Heidelberg. The trip had never proved particularly fruitful – third place was my best result there – and I suspected I might not be able to improve on that in '91. Hockenheim is a power circuit, with long straights punctuated by chicanes which come up to you very quickly, and a meandering section through the Stadium to complete the lap. It is a severe test of brakes, the aerodynamic package and above all, the engine. I felt it would again suit the McLaren Hondas.

It is a measure of the progress made by Williams and Renault that summer that we were able to outpace the McLarens all weekend. My engine on race day was excellent. I started from pole, led the race throughout and completed my first hat-trick of wins in Formula One. Riccardo came through to make it a marvellous one-two for Williams. I genuinely did not believe we were going to be that competitive, so it was a terrific boost. There was another bonus: Ayrton ran out of fuel again and the Championship gap was down to eight points.

In 1986 Formula One took the then fairly adventurous step into Eastern Europe, establishing a new venue near the Hungarian capital, Budapest. The Hungaroring, pleasantly situated in rolling countryside, is a track where pole position can win you the race. It's narrow, it winds up and down the hills, and it gives very little chance to overtake. It is also very demanding; the race is long and the weather here often hot. I was on pole for the 1987 race and on course for a convincing win when, five laps from the end, I was sabotaged by one of those more bizarre mishaps. The wheel nut came out of my right rear, the wheel tilted and all I could do was snake to an

Opposite First corner at the 1991 German Grand Prix. Mansell was uncatchable right from the start.

128

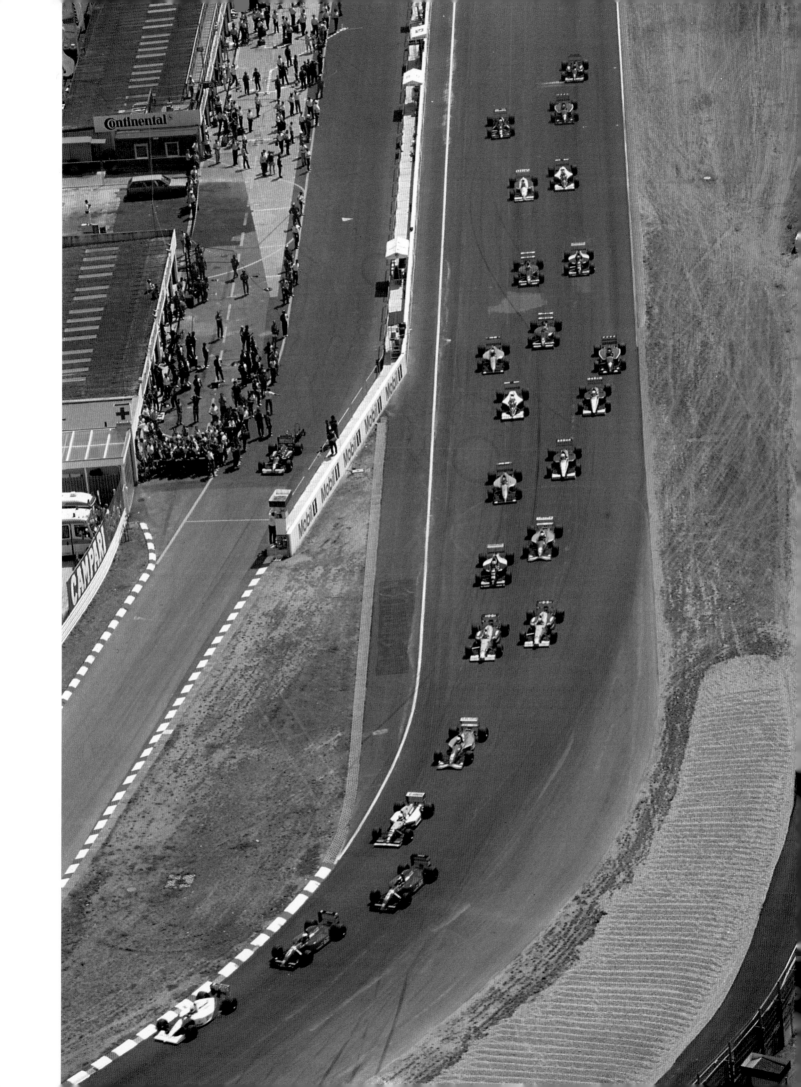

infuriating halt. I chased hard the following year, despite suffering the after-effects of chicken pox, but eventually exhaustion got the better of me and I had to retire.

There were those who thought I might as well have given in before the start of the 1989 Hungarian Grand Prix, lined up as I was, twelfth on the grid. That was the weekend when I deliberately gave up the chance of claiming a decent grid position to concentrate on finding a good race set-up. I wasn't at all happy with the front wing and knew we had to fix it. We did – and gained one-and-a-half seconds a lap. It was undoubtedly a calculated risk but, fortunately, I made the correct calculation.

I took four cars from the start, which obviously helped matters, yet it was just as much a day for patience as aggression. I attacked when I could and held back when I had to. By the fifty-third of the seventy-seven laps my steady advance had taken me up to second place. Ahead of me was Senna's McLaren. I closed up and on the fifty-eighth lap my opportunity came. Ayrton got so close to a backmarker (Stefan Johansson, in an Onyx), that although he moved right to overtake, he didn't have sufficient momentum to stop me taking them both as I went even wider to the right. I was able to consolidate my lead and secure my second success for Ferrari. It was a thinking man's win and has to go down as one of my best ever.

There was no fairytale ending to the race in 1991, when Ayrton had pole, held off Riccardo going into the first corner and then resisted my challenges later in the race. He had, effectively, won the day inside the first four or five seconds, demonstrating how important pole can be. McLaren had got their act together and were responding to the threat we represented. I had to battle for second place after three consecutive wins and Ayrton extended his title lead to twelve points.

Above On course for the eighth win of the season, Hockenheim, 1992. With Patrese leaving the track on the last lap, Mansell's lead widened, but the championship was still not secure.

Below A moment of relaxation with Sheridan Thynne, after second place in Hungary finally clinched the championship, 16 August 1992.

Above Mixed reflections of Budapest

Overleaf The twisting dilemma of the Hungaroring

Right Qualifying in the spare car, Hungary 1992, with number one mechanic Bob Davies.

Team talk, Hungary 1991

Opposite Centenarian, Austria, 1987

Very personal 38th birthday cake,
Hungary, 1991

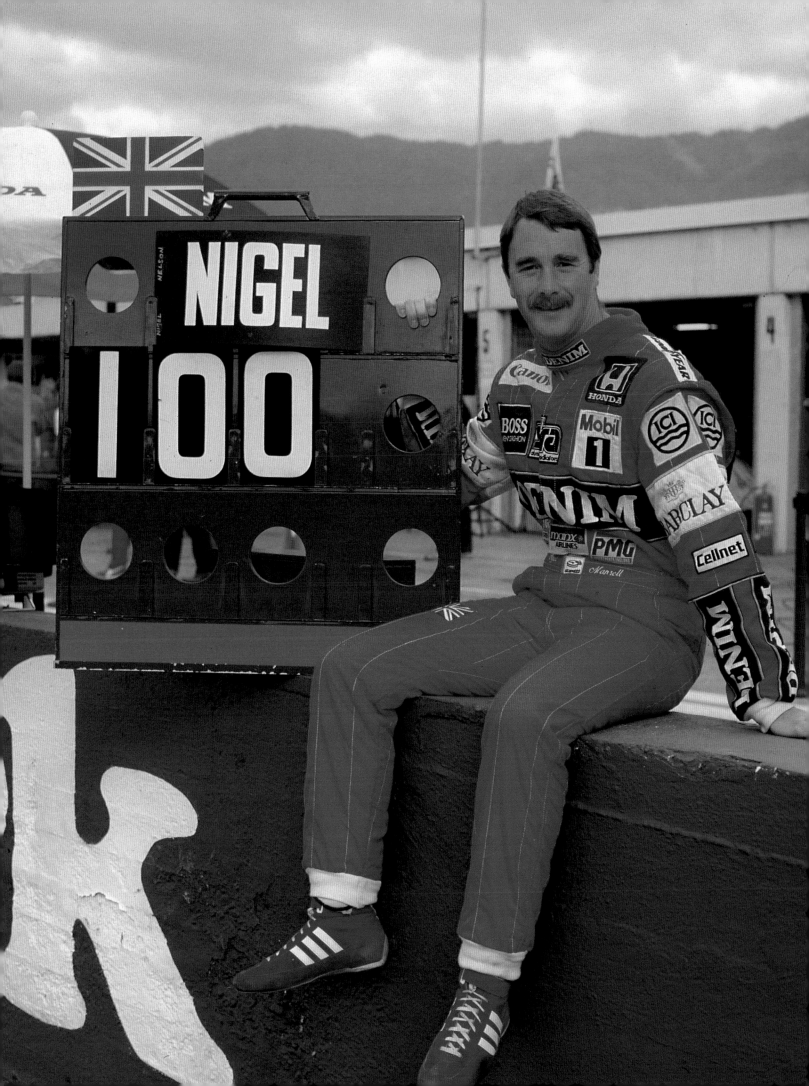

The summer tour around the central parts of Europe used to take us through Austria, calling at the magnificent Osterreichring. This was one of the super-fast circuits, with spectacular, tumbling sweeps through the forests. I had my Grand Prix debut there, in 1980, and also my hundredth appearance, in 1987. The celebration was perfect: victory. Sadly, we haven't been back!

We do, however, have a similarly spectacular circuit in Belgium. The Spa-Francorchamps track, at 4.312 miles the longest in Formula One, incorporates stretches of public road as it plunges up and down the Ardennes. It is a real test of the purist driver, with some breathtakingly quick sections – and some hairy ones. The drop down into and out of Eau Rouge – taken flat if you have the nerve – is one of the great sights in Grand Prix racing, although it was the focus of modification discussions following the 1991 race. The constant threat of changing weather conditions makes Spa even more daunting. I can recall occasions when we've had a perfectly dry road near the pits complex, and a downpour up at the top of the circuit. In 1985 the race was postponed because the track melted in the heat. It's that erratic.

My win in the 1986 Belgian Grand Prix put me on the Championship trail that season. The team was anxious about the fuel situation in the closing stages, warning me to contain my pace. I did just that and collected maximum points. I reckoned on doing the same the following year until an altercation with Senna put us both out of business for the day. The infamous

Above Celebratory victory at the 1987 Austrian Grand Prix

Opposite above Braking for the first corner of the 1991 Belgian Grand Prix

Opposite below Negotiating the chicane, Spa, 1991

Spectacular view of the
Spa-Francorchamps Circuit

Opposite The *tifosi* salute *Il Leone* at
Monza, 1991

rain greeted us in 1989, and I was third, behind the McLarens, after a terrific tussle with Prost. My second Belgian win looked safe in 1991. I hounded Ayrton during the early part of the race and, although he stubbornly resisted, time was on my side and I was content to sit there in second place until after the tyre stops. In the event, I didn't have to pass him because I came out of the pits with the advantage. The lads had done a fantastic job. It was probably our best pit stop of the year. Senna's crew, for once, didn't do so well and he dropped to fifth place. Fortunes were soon to change, however. An electrical failure forced me to stop, while Ayrton managed to move up the order and take the ten points. He now led by twenty-two points. It was a devastating blow to our Championship hopes.

The Italian Grand Prix is one of the high points of the season. Monza, just north of Milan, is one of the great arenas of any sport. It is a circuit of legends and unequalled passion. The supporters there are incredibly fanatical. Some may find the atmosphere here somewhat intimidating, but I find it inspiring. The invasion of the track at the end of a race is simply part of the tradition. This is a very special place and I yearned to get my first win there.

Monza is now the fastest circuit in Formula One, despite the chicanes. The two Lesmo corners are phenomenally demanding, the second one especially so. The Parabolica, a right-hander which propels the cars onto the straight, is another arduous test. A good balance is vital, but it's very much a case of finding a compromise. I'd had a second, third and fourth there before taking that final step to the top of the podium in 1991. It was one of my best races, a tremendously satisfying win and a very necessary one as far as my title aspirations were concerned. Anything less would have put the crown beyond reach, so I had to get it right.

It was a day to be tyre-conscious and, after following Ayrton for eighteen laps, I decided to wave Riccardo through and let him do the hounding. My team-mate warmed to the task and duly took Senna. Unfortunately, he was

Above Monza, fastest circuit in Formula One

Senna takes the lead at the start of the 1991 Italian Grand prix

Opposite Putting the pressure on Senna

One of the most satisfactory wins, Italy 1991

a little too quick going into the Ascari chicane a lap later and spun off. Having conserved my tyres I was able to step up my pace and put pressure on Ayrton. On the thirty-fourth lap I got the momentum coming out of the second Lesmo to pass. The sight from the victory rostrum as thousands of fans gathered below was terrific, and, although Ayrton still had an eighteen point cushion in the Championship, I wasn't going to let him rest.

The Portuguese Grand Prix has been one of the more eventful fixtures of my Formula One career. The pleasant, relaxing coastal area around Estoril provides an unlikely setting for a race which has a knack of producing drama and controversy. It has nothing like the passion and atmosphere of Monza, for instance, yet is a great race track, a driver's track, with that all-important long straight.

My first points at Estoril were scored in the torrential rain of 1985 after starting from the pit lane. The following season I was able to control proceedings from the front and claim the victory which gave me a ten-point lead in the Championship with two races remaining. I had to retire from the following two Portuguese events and in 1989 it all went horribly wrong for me just when it seemed nothing could get in the way of another win. Unfortunately, I slightly over-shot in the confusion of the pit stop and instinctively reversed, which was to earn me the black flag. By the time that was being shown, I was under Senna's rear wing, trying to relieve him of second place for the second time. I was driving into the sun and simply didn't see it. I attacked down the straight, Ayrton obviously didn't like being taken again and turned in. We collided and finished up in the gravel. Even after a hearing in Paris, FISA maintained I was culpable for not stopping under the black flag, and confirmed a 50,000-dollar fine and a one-race suspension. Although it was an unprecedented sanction, the authority

Opposite Out in front

142

Above Looking good at Estoril

insisted the decision had nothing to do with the fact that Senna's Championship chances had virtually disappeared.

Pole and victory were mine in 1990 and twelve months later I had my sights on a third Estoril success. Surely I'd had my bad experience there and nothing else could go wrong for me. I was fourth on the grid, made a positive, forceful start to go past Senna and Berger, and settled in behind Riccardo as we pulled clear. I took over at the front on the eighteenth lap, leaving us with only the pit stop to negotiate. I had barely drawn away from our pit when my right rear wheel came adrift, leaving me stranded in the outside lane. The gun man on that wheel had removed a cross-threaded nut and had not had a chance to replace it before I was sent off. The team, in their anxiety, set about fitting another wheel right there, in the fast lane. Work in that lane is prohibited for safety reasons and, eventually, I was shown the black flag.

By eventually I mean sixteen laps later, and during that time I had driven hard, climbing from seventeenth place to sixth. Our misdemeanour was apparently drawn to the attention of the stewards by at least one other team, but it seems to me that the whole episode was an absolute disgrace. Weren't we punished enough by losing a lap? Were we deliberately trying to cheat? And wouldn't it have been potentially more dangerous to try and drag the car across the pit lane before attaching the wheel? Not only was I cruelly denied the chance to compete for three or four valuable points, but Formula One was denied a closer Championship going into the final three rounds. That evening I trailed by twenty-four points.

Formula One is basking in its success in the land of the Rising Sun

Overleaf The distinctive figure-of-eight layout of the Suzuka Circuit

I have suffered the consequences of a whole catalogue of bizarre incidents in my career, incidents which might well have driven some people out of the sport, and that one really did bring me to my knees in exasperation. It was probably the most incredible of all. But the whole team was down and it was a time to stand by the lads, not apportion blame. A mistake was made, yet you can't say any single person was responsible. Things happen in the heat of the moment and, hard though it is to take, you have to accept that that's motor racing.

Suzuka, stage of the Japanese Grand Prix, has been reluctant to give me anything but pain and misery. The circuit, with a distinctive figure-of-eight lay-out, was added to the Championship schedule in 1987. It is the home of Honda and reflects the enormous following the sport has in Japan. Demand for tickets exceeds supply many-fold and fans start queuing for places the early morning of the day BEFORE the race. The enthusiasm is staggering.

I didn't actually race in 1987 because I badly damaged my back when I crashed during the first qualifying session. I also had to miss the final Grand Prix of that season, in Australia, and so lost my outside chance of the Championship. I started but didn't finish the next four races. In 1990, following the coming-together of Senna and Prost at the first corner, I led, only to be halted by a broken driveshaft. In 1991 I was the driver challenging Senna for the Championship. I had kept alive my slim hopes by winning in Barcelona but had to look for nothing less than another victory at Suzuka. McLaren and Honda had definitely got their act together that weekend and, despite committing everything to my qualifying effort, I lined up third on the grid, behind Berger and Senna.

The wheel of fortune finally turned against Nigel in Japan, 1991

It may be a fast-medium circuit, but it does not present many overtaking options, and McLaren set out to hold me off. Gerhard got away well and Ayrton protected his second place at the first corner. Gerhard quickly opened up a gap and, although I knew I could step up my pace, Ayrton had no intention of letting me through. If it stayed like this it would be good enough for him. I closed up through the corners but he was able to pull clear out of them. I tracked him into the right-hander at the start of the tenth lap and found myself sliding wide. I was into the gravel and my Championship campaign was over. I had no choice but to push and an unsympathetic brake pedal was having none of it. There was no reason for us to be dejected. We had given McLaren and Senna a good fight, and ensured Formula One a genuine Championship contest. I waited to offer the Champion my congratulations as he climbed from his car.

Adelaide has established itself as the last circuit of the Championship and is a worthy host for the end-of-term party. The Australians might have opted for a more obvious location for their Grand Prix, but this city had the initiative and the expertise to create what is now perhaps the most popular race among the Formula One fraternity. The Aussies love sport, love life and put on a super show. The race also gives me a chance to visit one of my sisters, Gail, who lives in Adelaide. She decided she had more chance of seeing me if she emigrated rather than stay in England!

It is the best of the street circuits. It has some demanding corners, a good complex of bends and a nice long, wide straight, so there are sensible passing opportunities. I wasn't too fond of that straight, the Brabham Straight, in 1986. I was driving along there at almost 200 mph when my

Opposite Suzuka, scene of another decisive race in 1991

Calm before the storm, Australia, 1991

rear left tyre blew. My Championship bid was also blown, though at the time my concern was to keep the car out of the wall. That much I achieved and I walked away uninjured. The pain was emotional and horrendous. Imagine, then, how I felt some time later when an official informed me that had I crashed into the wall I would have been champion, because they would have stopped the race. I didn't thank him for telling me that.

I was able to stay the Adelaide course for the first time in 1990, finishing second after a terrific scrap with Nelson Piquet's Benetton. The races in '89 and '91, however, were marred by heavy rain. The streets do not drain as well as they might and both events became farcical. The '89 Grand Prix was bad enough, but two years later it was worse still. Even if the officials were justified in starting the race, it should have been stopped long before the red flag appeared. By then there were broken cars littering the main straight and a recovery truck parked on the track. The spray made it a nightmare and when I moved out to attack Senna for the lead I was astonished to see wreckage ahead of me. I was eventually thrown into the wall and was perhaps fortunate I had nothing worse than a damaged foot. Cars were going off everywhere. Wisely, they did not restart the race, so the final positions were taken at the end of the fourteenth lap – making it the shortest Grand Prix in the history of the World Championship – and I had second place. That gave me a total of seventy-two points for the season and runner-up position, twenty-four points behind Ayrton.

It was a great shame a fine season should have been concluded in such disarray. I suggested to Bernie Ecclestone that we ought to consider taking a leaf out of the American book and introduce pace cars, an idea which has been taken on board. Safety procedures need to be kept under constant

Wading through the rain of Adelaide

The 1991 Australian Grand Prix is mercifully halted

review, and tracks must be updated regularly to stay in line with the development of Formula One cars.

Overleaf Smile, please, ... the 1991 driver line-up

The Opposition

*F*ormula One is the top echelon of a sport in which many thousands participate every week, all round the world. At the lower levels are amateur enthusiasts who race simply for fun and have no ambitions to join the ranks of the professionals. Those who do aspire to greater things are confronted with a steep, slippery slope. They may realize, halfway up, that Formula Three, or Formula 3000, or perhaps sportscars or saloons, will mark the limit of their capabilities. Many will dream of Formula One, whether or not they have good reason to. Most of these will come sliding back down that slope. Some, through money and influence, will succeed in hitching a chair lift to the upper peaks. But those who reach the pinnacle, join the very best teams and stay there, generally do so on merit. They have the ability, dedication and a head for Formula One heights.

People do not complete that long, arduous climb by accident. Those who do are, by definition, talented, competitive, single-minded, even ruthless. Mental toughness is as important as fundamental skills. Experience moulds the qualities into place so it is no coincidence that the drivers who have regularly won races in recent seasons have been those in their thirties.

When I first came into Formula One with Lotus, in 1980, the man on his way to the World Championship was driving a Williams. That man was Alan Jones. Here was a hard, no-nonsense Aussie who carried the spirit of Williams on to the track. Even then, when they were my opponents, I was struck by the combative, racing force which was so much a feature of the team. It stemmed, as we have discussed, from Frank and Patrick, and Alan was of like mind and attitude. He was almost made for the job, the perfect man to lead this bold, unpretentious outfit to their first title. Alan was probably underestimated by a lot of people until he earned the Williams' drive (haven't I heard that one before?), but once there he showed what a great driver he was. Alan could be brash and always called a spade a spade, but although he was also tough and aggressive on the track, his judgement and race craft were very sound. He made an enormous impression on me.

Williams had a similar sort of character in Keke Rosberg after Jones left the team. Keke, a Finn, had been scratching around the smaller teams, trying to show what he could do, and was given his chance with Williams in 1982. He made the most of the chance, winning the Championship that year through consistency. The turbos were gathering strength but the trusty old Ford Cosworth engine finished races. Keke had only one win that season – in the conveniently arranged Swiss Grand Prix at Dijon – yet scored sufficiently well throughout the season to clinch the title.

Opposite Alan Jones celebrates victory at Long Beach, 1981, flanked by Carlos Reutemann and Nelson Piquet

155

Keke Rosberg, 'my best team-mate', 1985

That success proved his ability to do a solid management job, but Keke will always be remembered for his flamboyant style. He was a terrific entertainer. He seemed so laid back off the track, but then he'd put out his cigarette, climb into the cockpit and throw the car all over the place. He was an instinctive driver, another typical Williams racer.

In the early days Keke made no secret of the fact that he did not have a high opinion of me. He harangued me over my driving tactics after the 1984 Dallas Grand Prix and told everyone he didn't want me in the team the following year. Frank quietly reminded him who was running the team and signed me. The atmosphere was a little tense to start with, but once we got down to work there was a noticeable change in Keke's attitude. Soon we became firm friends, and there is no question he was the best team-mate I ever had. He admitted he'd been wrong about me, explaining that he'd been fed poisonous propaganda before I joined Williams. You knew where you stood with Keke. He was straight, a great guy.

Another great crowd pleaser was, of course, Gilles Villeneuve, the French-Canadian killed in qualifying for the 1982 Belgian Grand Prix at Zolder. He was such an exciting driver, sometimes daring to the point of being outrageous. His cavalier style inevitably appealed to the Italians, and he became a Ferrari folk hero. When I joined Ferrari I felt it was a great privilege to bear the number '27' Gilles made famous.

Dreams are often broken at Ferrari but one man who made it work there was Niki Lauda. He was an extremely gifted driver and a great tactician both on and off the track. He made sure he got the team around him and for him, the significance of which I was to appreciate to the full when I

Gilles Villeneuve, loved by the Ferrari fans, 1982

went to Maranello. Niki knew his mind. He was strong-willed and wouldn't be pushed around. He courageously came back after suffering appalling burns in a crash at the Nurburgring in 1976, but showed just as much courage when he climbed out of the car at a wet Fuji later that year because his vision was affected, and again when he walked away from Formula One in 1979. I raced against him when he came back in 1982, with McLaren. In 1984, when McLaren won twelve races, he pipped his team-mate, Alain Prost, by half a point to win his third world title. He wasn't as fast as Alain and often started down the grid, but he was as cunning as a fox, knew how to poach and how to get what he wanted. Alain no doubt learned a lot from his first-hand experience of working with Niki.

I found myself in the Championship contest for the first time in 1986, when the other contenders were Prost, of McLaren, Ayrton Senna, who was with Lotus, and Nelson Piquet, my new team-mate at Williams. They were to remain great rivals for some time, as Ayrton and I, of course, have been up to the present era. We have all had our battles, and we have undeniably had our differences, but no-one should ever lose sight of the fact that here we are talking about drivers a notch above the best of the rest. Like Jones, Rosberg, Lauda and Villeneuve, they are in a league of their own. Prost, Piquet and Senna are all triple champions. They are winners.

Niki Lauda, master on and off the track,
1984

They have the turn of speed and the commitment to succeed. Any comments I make about the three men who have been my fiercest opponents are relative. We are dealing here with the best in the business.

Nelson clearly didn't think he would be dealing with one of the best in the business when he signed for Williams, late in the summer of 1985. I hadn't won a race at that stage and he was to have number one status in 1986. He was, after all, a double champion. Before the end of the '85 season, however, I won two races and looked forward to still more success the following season. By the summer of '86 I was, indeed, enjoying more success. I was winning races and had emerged as a genuine threat to his or anyone else's Championship plans. There's no doubt I had taken Nelson and many others by surprise. I wasn't generally expected to have the pace or consistency to beat him, he'd had an unchallenged reign at Brabham and this was a totally new experience for him.

He began to complain that the team were displaying favouritism towards their British driver, an accusation Frank dismissed as nonsense. The following year, when the Championship was really between the two of us, the situation worsened, and our relationship deteriorated further. Without a drive going into the 1992 season, he subsequently announced his retirement from Formula One racing. A serious injury while racing in America, jeopardizing his eventual return to the sport, underlines its dangers at all levels.

Despite the antagonism, I willingly acknowledge that Nelson has been one of the outstanding drivers of his time, with a nice style and feel for the car. He always liked fast, flowing circuits but, as he showed against me at Adelaide, in 1990, he could also put up a fight on street circuits. When he'd got the taste for a fight he was a hard man to beat. In the competitive stakes he was probably somewhere between Alain and Ayrton. He was a tougher opponent than Alain if not quite as tough as Ayrton.

I always had great admiration for Alain, a driver with all-round ability and a record that speaks for itself: an unprecedented forty-four Grand Prix wins as well as three Championships. For a long time I regarded him as a good friend, we got on well and frequently played golf together. It is no secret that the relationship turned sour after he became my team-mate at Ferrari, in 1990.

I'd had a good first year at Ferrari, winning a couple of races, and looked nicely set up for a Championship challenge in 1990. I was to have outright number one status and signed a contract to that effect. Then, when Alain became available I, and others inside Ferrari, were put under pressure to bring him on board. They naturally had to buy out clauses in my contract to assure him joint number one status, and I felt that I could trust Alain, work with him and form a partnership to beat McLaren. However, I had no real choice in the matter, and a refusal to co-operate would have been counter-productive. They were determined to have him so it was best to go along with them. I had no control over the situation, so I have no regrets over my course of action.

The problem for me was that Ferrari seemed to think they had got something better in Alain and apparently allowed him to have his own way.

Alain Prost, relationship turned sour

The legendary Prancing Horse

Personnel came and went and, although I could have stayed, it would have meant playing second fiddle, and I had no intention of doing that. It was a classic case of Ferrari self-destructing, as was to become apparent in 1991. They had turned in the wrong direction and were to pay very heavily for it, losing their leading edge among the teams at the top of Formula One, and much to the disappointment of their millions of fans. Alain and they eventually parted company.

Ferrari give you the world but expect you to deliver in return, and rightly so. I am proud of the fact that I departed from the team on good terms and I've always been welcome in the camp since. I learned an awful lot and gained a great deal of confidence from my experience with Ferrari. The Ferrari mystique is still an enormously powerful force. It is the team every driver should want to drive for at some stage of his career. The down-side is that the team is such a hive of political intrigue, that too often, instead of getting on with the job, individuals become side-tracked by internal squabbles and disagreements. As a result they have spent vast amounts of money going down the wrong route. They need to have a very clear direction, believe in it, support it and stick with it. Only then can they hope to return to the top of Formula One.

Alain presumably thought he could give them that direction but the only race in which they were genuinely competitive during 1991 was the French Grand Prix. That was where I passed him twice at the same corner, first on the inside, then on the outside. Two or three weeks later he told me that had really annoyed him, while I found it hard to believe I had actually got away with it. But then I think Alain does, perhaps, lack something when it comes to RACING. He is an extremely smooth, precise, technical driver, and his pace should never be underestimated. But things seem to have to be just right for Alain. He openly detests street circuits and rain, and is far from happy negotiating traffic. He is certainly not as aggressive or alert, in attack or defence, as some other drivers.

I don't think, for example, that I would have caught Ayrton napping twice, the way I caught out Alain at Magny-Cours that day. I suspect Ayrton would have computed that I might try the outside after pulling off that manoeuvre inside. Every driver thinks differently and you have to work out ways of out-witting each of them. You build up a mental catalogue of the other drivers, of their strengths and weaknesses, and of where you should or should not try to take them on.

Senna is not an easy man to out-race or out-think and we have had some tremendous battles against each other. We both know the score when we're racing. We're both hard and if either tries something stupid the other will 'slam the door' on him. With Senna you have to be totally committed to race wheel to wheel with him. Against a lesser driver you might be able to hold back a little, but not with Ayrton; if you do, you simply play into his hands.

How good is Senna? There is no disputing that he's a tremendous driver: fast, competitive, committed, a true racer. He may be one of the all-time greats, but if he is then maybe I am one of the new greats. Given equal equipment, I would always be happy to take him on. Over the years, he has tended to have the best package in McLaren Honda, and the total support of the organization. He has, however, done a fantastic job with that package and all credit for that is due to him.

He seems, though, to become rattled when under pressure. He made a big fuss about my driving at the start of the 1991 Portuguese Grand Prix, saying I was too hard, which was something, coming from Ayrton! Not

Ayrton Senna and his other love, model aircraft

content with that, he launched an extraordinary verbal attack on me at that eventful drivers' briefing before the race in Barcelona, a week later. The more insulting he became the bigger compliment he paid me because it was obvious he was worried about my speed and the way I was pushing him in the World Championship. After my win in Spain he appeared even more upset.

This is a common characteristic of anyone who has been used to having everything his own way. It is easy to be the most popular person in the world when everything is going to plan and Ayrton was very friendly in Australia once he'd won the title.

Any aggravation between us of late has tended to be one-sided. A certain amount of mud has come this way but I have tried to resist returning it in kind. It was coming from Ayrton because I was challenging him and he isn't used to it. I won't give way to him as so many others do, I'll stand up to him, as I've demonstrated to him and to others time and time again. We've beaten each other a fair number of times over the years and our acknowledged rivalry on the track has brought spice and excitement to many races.

Everyone in every walk of life – not just Formula One – has a certain amount of pride, maybe even ego. They have their own satisfaction level, their own targets. The very best drivers are ultra-competitive people at the peak of their powers, who will always want to aim high, so it's inevitable that rivalry will be intense and friction may well be a consequence. Manufacturers and sponsors also enter the fray. This is big business as well as a highly competitive sporting contest and the pressure on the drivers can come from many sides.

Outright antagonism, however, is unacceptable. There have been well-documented 'conflicts' down the years: there was no love lost between Alan Jones and Nelson Piquet, or between Alan and one of his team-mates at Williams, Carlos Reutemann; Nelson and I weren't exactly bosom buddies, nor were Alain and I after a year at Ferrari. The most notorious clash of all was that between Alain and Ayrton, and, knowing both of them, that came as no surprise to me at all.

But rivalry should be kept in perspective. A little friction here, or a word out of place there does not amount to open warfare. This is a high profile, high pressure game and the stakes are high, too. People should not necessarily be held accountable for things that are done and said in the heat of the moment, when the adrenalin is pumping and the nerves are stretched. Often incidents are built up out of all proportion. I have no doubt that attempts are made to aggravate the situation between Ayrton and me, for instance. One of us may make an innocuous comment about the other, a journalist will pick it up and then say to the other 'Did you hear what he said?', and suddenly there's a so-called slanging match between us when, in truth, there is nothing of the sort. It's just a manufactured 'story'. Basically we respect each other. We have been racing against each other for a good many years, often right at the front of the field, head-to-head. I'd like to think that when we've finished racing people might look back and say 'Yes, they were good value, those two.'

There is, I believe, a lot of quality in Formula One, and I need look no further than my own team-mate, Riccardo Patrese, for evidence of that. Riccardo has competed in more Grands Prix than any other driver in the history of the World Championship and has improved with experience. Over the last year or two he has been particularly strong. On his day, he can be tremendously quick and he is a tough, dogged competitor. It has often been said of Riccardo that he lacks consistency and that he allows his Italian temperament to get the better of him, but he has gained consistency and seems to have enjoyed the chance to demonstrate his ability in recent seasons.

Ayrton's partner, Gerhard Berger, is also a highly talented driver. He has pace, courage and lots of aggression. He likes a fight and isn't afraid to bang wheels from time to time. Towards the end of the 1991 season we saw Gerhard at his best, out-qualifying and sometimes out-racing Ayrton, showing what he could do when he got the equipment. McLaren and Honda clearly identified Ayrton as the better bet for the Championship so Gerhard has had something of an uphill struggle at times. He has continued to demonstrate his ability during the 1992 season, but he does seem to have difficulty sustaining form. Perhaps that will come with more experience, as it did for Riccardo. I drove with Gerhard for a season at Ferrari and I wondered about his concentration. There were also times when I suspected he tried to push a little too hard and possibly over-stretched himself. That weekend of his big accident at Imola (which I must stress was through no fault of his but a failure on the car) he was visibly straining on the circuit to the point of being ragged.

Gerhard was a good team-mate, colleague and friend, and I'd like to think we are still pals. The skirmish at Barcelona was a bit of nonsense which can be dismissed as no more than that. Gerhard just happens to have a sense of humour which sometimes gets the better of him. Often the joke can be shared and certainly you must have a few laughs even when it's at your expense. The ability to see the funny side of any situation is particularly important in a sport as potentially dangerous as ours, when tensions can

Shake, partner, with Riccardo Patrese

Below Riccardo Patrese, most
experienced driver in Formula One

Gerhard Berger, former team mate

build quickly and disturbed concentration be disastrous. Yet, if, occasionally, Gerhard's pranks go a little too far, I am sure much of his behaviour may be put down to frustration, and the pressure of being with McLaren, Honda, Marlboro and Ayrton, must be considerable.

Jean Alesi found himself in a difficult situation when he joined Ferrari as Prost's team-mate. He earned all sorts of rave reviews when he appeared on the Formula One scene with Tyrrell. Here was a gifted, precocious, ambitious young man who made it plain he didn't intend to be intimidated by reputations. He is also an example of a promising young driver being built up far too much, far too soon. The praise and pressure were too much. He'd been around for only two minutes, he needed time to learn and develop. I like Jean and I hope he gets the time and space he needs.

Much the same situation confronts the latest 'overnight sensation' of Formula One, Michael Schumacher. He made a terrific impact when he came in with Jordan at the 1991 Belgian Grand Prix and after his controversial move to Benetton for the next race, in Italy. He scored his first points there and was in brilliant form from the start of the 1992 season. There's no question that he is an outstanding talent. He is a very quick, instinctive driver and has the confidence, even in his early twenties, to take on anyone, but he needs to understand why he is quick and learn to pull back a little when the circumstances require him to do so. Youthful enthusiasm and exuberance are wonderful to see, but bravado can be a dangerous trait. He had a few accidents in his early race meetings. Even as

Jean Alesi, unfair pressure

Michael Schumacher, star of the future

he was having one of these, during qualifying in Japan, he refused to lift off the power and was very lucky to get out of the car uninjured.

Michael is another young driver I have a lot of time for. I'd like to see him stay in Formula One a long time and fulfil his potential because he undoubtedly has the ability to be one of the stars of the future. Michael and I have actually discussed this and I have tried to help him because all young drivers need guidance. I would have appreciated a bit of friendly advice every now and then when I was young but it was never forthcoming.

We need to help and encourage our youngsters in Britain as much as possible without, as I said earlier, putting them under undue pressure. We have long had a situation in Formula One whereby drivers get seats through commercial or political influence. The world-wide recession of recent times has resulted in even more 'bought drives'. This is a business as well as a sport and some of the smaller teams have to do what they can to generate funds. It would certainly appear that the standards and qualifications required to attain a super licence are not what they were, and to some of the drivers left out in the cold it must seem terribly unfair. British drivers, unfortunately, find themselves in the middle of this tough situation. Our test driver, Damon Hill, and McLaren's test driver, Mark Blundell, are two who are entitled to consider themselves unlucky not to have secured Formula One drives for the start of 1992.

Another Englishman sadly out of Formula One is Derek Warwick. He should never have been allowed to leave. I'm not just saying this because

Derek is a friend and missed by everyone but because, as we can all see, there are drivers of lesser calibre currently in Grand Prix cars. However, these are also the drivers who bring along sponsorship of three or four or five million dollars, and with money getting scarcer a manufacturer or team owner can't really be blamed for taking the driver with the bag of gold. This syndrome is something we have to live with, but it is consoling to know the top drives still can't be bought, and that, eventually, ability is the key factor. The trouble is that Williams, McLaren and Ferrari look very distant when you are starting and, unless you are given the opportunity to show what you can do, you can't even think of driving for these front-line teams.

In my Formula One career I have had the thrill and privilege of driving for three of the greatest teams in the history of the sport. Unlike Williams and Ferrari, however, Lotus have not been in the big league in recent seasons, and it has been sad to see them going through such a difficult period. When Colin Chapman died, Lotus virtually died. Colin was the man who built and inspired Lotus; he made them the power they were. Now my old pal Peter Collins is doing a fantastic job trying to resurrect Team Lotus and I wish him well. It would be marvellous to see Lotus up at the front of the grid again, competing for the Championship, but Peter knows better than anyone that it is going to be a long, tough road back.

The one team who seem certain to remain in direct opposition for the forseeable future are McLaren. Ron Dennis, their managing director, runs a superb operation and he has always had the sponsorship and engine deal to complete the package. He had Porsche and, since 1988, he has had Honda. Ron once asked to speak to me about the possibility of a drive for 1987 but at the time I was under immense pressure from, ironically, Honda, to stay with Williams. That weekend, at Hockenheim, I struck a deal with Williams, so I never got round to serious negotiations with Ron.

Now I'm back with Williams and McLaren are still the opposition. We had no illusions about that when we embarked upon the 1992 season. The challenge beckoned. So, too, we hoped, did the Championship.

Overleaf Monaco 1992

Opposite Derek Warwick, should be in Formula One

Opposite left Mark Blundell, deserves drive

Opposite right Peter Collins, reviving Lotus

Victory in Brazil marked the third consecutive win of the 1992 season, giving Nigel maximum points.

Nigel Mansell's Formula One Record

TEAM: LOTUS

1980

AUSTRIA   *Qualifying*: 24th. *Race*: retired.
HOLLAND   *Qualifying*: 16th. *Race*: retired.
ITALY   Did not qualify.

1981

USA, LONG BEACH   *Qualifying*: 7th. *Race*: retired.
BRAZIL   *Qualifying*: 13th. *Race*: 11th.
ARGENTINA   *Qualifying*: 15th. *Race*: retired.
SAN MARINO   Entry withdrawn.
BELGIUM   *Qualifying*: 10th. *Race*: 3rd.
MONACO   *Qualifying*: 3rd. *Race*: retired.
SPAIN   *Qualifying*: 11th. *Race*: 6th.
FRANCE   *Qualifying*: 13th. *Race*: 7th.
BRITAIN   Did not qualify.
GERMANY   *Qualifying*: 15th. *Race*: retired.
AUSTRIA   *Qualifying*: 11th. *Race*: retired.
HOLLAND   *Qualifying*: 17th, placed 16th on grid after De Cesaris withdrawn. *Race*: retired.
ITALY   *Qualifying*: 12th. *Race*: retired.
CANADA   *Qualifying*: 5th. *Race*: retired.
USA, LAS VEGAS   *Qualifying*: 9th. *Race*: 4th. Non-Championship
SOUTH AFRICA   *Qualifying*: 8th. *Race*: 10th.

1982

SOUTH AFRICA   *Qualifying*: 18th. *Race*: retired.
BRAZIL   *Qualifying*: 14th. *Race*: 5th, placed 3rd after two drivers disqualified.
USA, LONG BEACH   *Qualifying*: 17th. *Race*: 7th.
SAN MARINO   Entry withdrawn.
BELGIUM   *Qualifying*: 7th. *Race*: retired.
MONACO   *Qualifying*: 11th. *Race*: 4th.
USA, DETROIT   *Qualifying*: 7th. *Race*: retired.
CANADA   *Qualifying*: 14th. *Race*: retired.

HOLLAND   Entry withdrawn.
BRITAIN   *Qualifying*: 23rd. *Race*: retired.
FRANCE   Entry withdrawn.
GERMANY   *Qualifying*: 17th. *Race*: 9th.
AUSTRIA   *Qualifying*: 12th. *Race*: retired.
SWISS (DIJON, FRANCE)   *Qualifying*: 26th. *Race*: 8th.
ITALY   *Qualifying*: 23rd. *Race*: 7th.
USA, LAS VEGAS   *Qualifying*: 21st. *Race*: retired.

1983

BRAZIL   *Qualifying*: 22nd. *Race*: 12th.
USA, LONG BEACH   *Qualifying*: 13th. *Race*: 12th.
FRANCE   *Qualifying*: 18th. *Race*: retired.
SAN MARINO   *Qualifying*: 15th. *Race*: retired.
MONACO   *Qualifying*: 13th. *Race*: retired.
BELGIUM   *Qualifying*: 19th. *Race*: retired.
USA, DETROIT   *Qualifying*: 14th. *Race*: 6th.
CANADA   *Qualifying*: 18th. *Race*: retired.
BRITAIN   *Qualifying*: 18th. *Race*: 4th.
GERMANY   *Qualifying*: 17th. *Race*: retired.
AUSTRIA   *Qualifying*: 3rd. *Race*: 5th.
HOLLAND   *Qualifying*: 5th. *Race*: retired.
ITALY   *Qualifying*: 11th. *Race*: 8th.
EUROPE (BRANDS HATCH)   *Qualifying*: 3rd. *Race*: 3rd.
SOUTH AFRICA   *Qualifying*: 7th. *Race*: Not classified.

1984

BRAZIL   *Qualifying*: 5th. *Race*: retired.
SOUTH AFRICA   *Qualifying*: 3rd. *Race*: retired.
BELGIUM   *Qualifying*: 10th. *Race*: retired.
SAN MARINO   *Qualifying*: 18th. *Race*: retired.
FRANCE   *Qualifying*: 6th. *Race*: 3rd.
MONACO   *Qualifying*: 2nd. *Race*: retired.
CANADA   *Qualifying*: 7th. *Race*: 6th.
USA, DETROIT   *Qualifying*: 3rd. *Race*: retired.
USA, DALLAS   *Qualifying*: 1st. *Race*: 6th.
BRITAIN   *Qualifying*: 8th. *Race*: retired.
GERMANY   *Qualifying*: 16th. *Race*: 4th.

AUSTRIA   *Qualifying*: 8th. *Race*: retired.
HOLLAND   *Qualifying*: 12th. *Race*: 3rd.
ITALY   *Qualifying*: 7th. *Race*: retired.
EUROPE (NURBURGRING)   *Qualifying*: 8th. *Race*: retired.
PORTUGAL   *Qualifying*: 6th. *Race*: retired.

TEAM: WILLIAMS

1985

BRAZIL   *Qualifying*: 5th. *Race*: retired.
PORTUGAL   *Qualifying*: 9th, pit lane start. *Race*: 5th.
SAN MARINO   *Qualifying*: 7th. *Race*: 5th.
MONACO   *Qualifying*: 2nd. *Race*: 7th.
CANADA   *Qualifying*: 16th. *Race*: 6th.
USA, DETROIT   *Qualifying*: 2nd. *Race*: retired.
FRANCE   withdrew.
BRITAIN   *Qualifying*: 5th. *Race*: retired.
GERMANY   *Qualifying*: 10th. *Race*: 6th.
AUSTRIA   *Qualifying*: 2nd. *Race*: retired.
HOLLAND   *Qualifying*: 7th. *Race*: 6th.
ITALY   *Qualifying*: 3rd. *Race*: retired.
BELGIUM   *Qualifying*: 7th. *Race*: 2nd.
EUROPE (BRANDS HATCH)   *Qualifying*: 3rd. *Race*: 1st.
SOUTH AFRICA   *Qualifying*: 1st. *Race*: 1st.
AUSTRALIA   *Qualifying*: 2nd. *Race*: retired.

1986

BRAZIL   *Qualifying*: 3rd. *Race*: retired.
SPAIN   *Qualifying*: 3rd. *Race*: 2nd.
SAN MARINO   *Qualifying*: 3rd. *Race*: retired.
MONACO   *Qualifying*: 2nd. *Race*: 4th.
BELGIUM   *Qualifying*: 5th. *Race*: 1st.
CANADA   *Qualifying*: 1st. *Race*: 1st.
USA, DETROIT   *Qualifying*: 2nd. *Race*: 5th.
FRANCE   *Qualifying*: 2nd. *Race*: 1st.
BRITAIN   *Qualifying*: 2nd. *Race*: 1st.
GERMANY   *Qualifying*: 6th. *Race*: 3rd.
HUNGARY   *Qualifying*: 4th. *Race*: 3rd.
AUSTRIA   *Qualifying*: 6th. *Race*: retired.
ITALY   *Qualifying*: 3rd. *Race*: 2nd.
PORTUGAL   *Qualifying*: 2nd. *Race*: 1st.
MEXICO   *Qualifying*: 3rd. *Race*: 5th.
AUSTRALIA   *Qualifying*: 1st. *Race*: retired.

1987

BRAZIL   *Qualifying*: 1st. *Race*: 6th.
SAN MARINO   *Qualifying*: 2nd. *Race*: 1st.
BELGIUM   *Qualifying*: 1st. *Race*: retired.
MONACO   *Qualifying*: 1st. *Race*: retired.
USA, DETROIT   *Qualifying*: 1st. *Race*: 5th.
FRANCE   *Qualifying*: 1st. *Race*: 1st.

BRITAIN   *Qualifying*: 2nd. *Race*: 1st.
GERMANY   *Qualifying*: 1st. *Race*: retired.
HUNGARY   *Qualifying*: 1st. *Race*: retired.
AUSTRIA   *Qualifying*: 2nd. *Race*: 1st.
ITALY   *Qualifying*: 2nd. *Race*: 3rd.
PORTUGAL   *Qualifying*: 2nd. *Race*: retired.
SPAIN   *Qualifying*: 2nd. *Race*: 1st.
MEXICO   *Qualifying*: 1st. *Race*: 1st.
JAPAN   Withdrew.
AUSTRALIA   Entry withdrawn.

1988

BRAZIL   *Qualifying*: 2nd. *Race*: retired.
SAN MARINO   *Qualifying*: 11th. *Race*: retired.
MONACO   *Qualifying*: 5th. *Race*: retired.
MEXICO   *Qualifying*: 14th. *Race*: retired.
CANADA   *Qualifying*: 9th. *Race*: retired.
USA, DETROIT   *Qualifying*: 6th. *Race*: retired.
FRANCE,   *Qualifying*: 9th. *Race*: retired.
BRITAIN   *Qualifying*: 11th. *Race*: 2nd.
GERMANY   *Qualifying*: 11th. *Race*: retired.
HUNGARY   *Qualifying*: 2nd. *Race*: retired.
BELGIUM   Entry withdrawn.
ITALY   Entry withdrawn.
PORTUGAL   *Qualifying*: 6th. *Race*: retired.
SPAIN   *Qualifying*: 3rd. *Race*: 2nd.
JAPAN   *Qualifying*: 8th. *Race*: retired.
AUSTRALIA   *Qualifying*: 3rd. *Race*: retired.

TEAM: FERRARI

1989

BRAZIL   *Qualifying*: 6th. *Race*: 1st.
SAN MARINO   *Qualifying*: 3rd. *Race*: retired.
MONACO   *Qualifying*: 5th. *Race*: retired.
MEXICO   *Qualifying*: 3rd. *Race*: retired.
USA, PHEONIX   *Qualifying*: 4th. *Race*: retired.
CANADA   *Qualifying*: 5th. *Race*: disqualified.
FRANCE   *Qualifying*: 3rd, pit lane start. *Race*: 2nd.
BRITAIN   *Qualifying*: 3rd. *Race*: 2nd.
GERMANY   *Qualifying*: 3rd. *Race*: 3rd.
HUNGARY   *Qualifying*: 12th. *Race*: 1st.
BELGIUM   *Qualifying*: 6th. *Race*: 3rd.
ITALY   *Qualifying*: 3rd. *Race*: retired.
PORTUGAL   *Qualifying*: 3rd. *Race*: disqualified.
SPAIN, JEREZ   Suspended.
JAPAN   *Qualifying*: 4th. *Race*: retired.
AUSTRALIA   *Qualifying*: 7th. *Race*: retired.

1990

USA, PHOENIX   *Qualifying*: 17th. *Race*: retired.
BRAZIL   *Qualifying*: 5th. *Race*: 4th.

SAN MARINO   *Qualifying*: 5th. *Race*: retired.
MONACO   *Qualifying*: 7th. *Race*: retired.
CANADA   *Qualifying*: 7th. *Race*: 3rd.
MEXICO   *Qualifying*: 4th. *Race*: 2nd.
FRANCE   *Qualifying*: 1st. *Race*: retired.
BRITAIN   *Qualifying*: 1st. *Race*: retired.
GERMANY   *Qualifying*: 4th. *Race*: retired.
HUNGARY   *Qualifying*: 5th. *Race*: retired.
BELGIUM   *Qualifying*: 5th. *Race*: retired.
ITALY   *Qualifying*: 4th. *Race*: 4th.
PORTUGAL   *Qualifying*: 1st. *Race*: 1st.
SPAIN   *Qualifying*: 3rd. *Race*: 2nd.
JAPAN   *Qualifying*: 3rd. *Race*: retired.
AUSTRALIA   *Qualifying*: 3rd. *Race*: 2nd.

TEAM: WILLIAMS

1991

USA, PHOENIX   *Qualifying:* 4th. *Race*: retired.
BRAZIL   *Qualifying*: 3rd. *Race*: retired.
SAN MARINO   *Qualifying*: 4th. *Race*: retired.
MONACO   *Qualifying*: 5th. *Race*: 2nd.
CANADA   *Qualifying*: 2nd. *Race*: 6th.
MEXICO   *Qualifying*: 2nd. *Race*: 2nd.
FRANCE   *Qualifying*: 4th. *Race*: 1st.

BRITAIN   *Qualifying*: 1st. *Race*: 1st.
GERMANY   *Qualifying*: 1st. *Race*: 1st.
HUNGARY   *Qualifying*: 3rd. *Race*: 2nd.
BELGIUM   *Qualifying*: 3rd. *Race*: retired.
ITALY   *Qualifying*: 2nd. *Race*: 1st.
PORTUGAL   *Qualifying*: 4th. *Race*: disqualified.
SPAIN   *Qualifying*: 2nd. *Race*: 1st.
JAPAN   *Qualifying*: 3rd. *Race*: retired.
AUSTRALIA   *Qualifying*: 3rd. *Race*: 2nd.

1992

SOUTH AFRICA   *Qualifying*: 1st. *Race*: 1st.
MEXICO   *Qualifying*: 1st. *Race*: 1st.
BRAZIL   *Qualifying*: 1st. *Race*: 1st.
SPAIN   *Qualifying*: 1st. *Race*: 1st.
SAN MARINO   *Qualifying*: 1st. *Race*: 1st.
MONACO   *Qualifying*: 1st. *Race*: 2nd.
CANADA   *Qualifying*: 3rd. *Race*: retired.
FRANCE   *Qualifying*: 1st. *Race*: 1st.
BRITAIN   *Qualifying*: 1st. *Race*: 1st.
GERMANY   *Qualifying*: 1st. *Race*: 1st.
HUNGARY   *Qualifying*: 2nd. *Race*: 2nd.
BELGIUM   *Qualifying*:
ITALY   *Qualifying*:
PORTUGAL   *Qualifying*:
JAPAN   *Qualifying*:
AUSTRALIA   *Qualifying*:

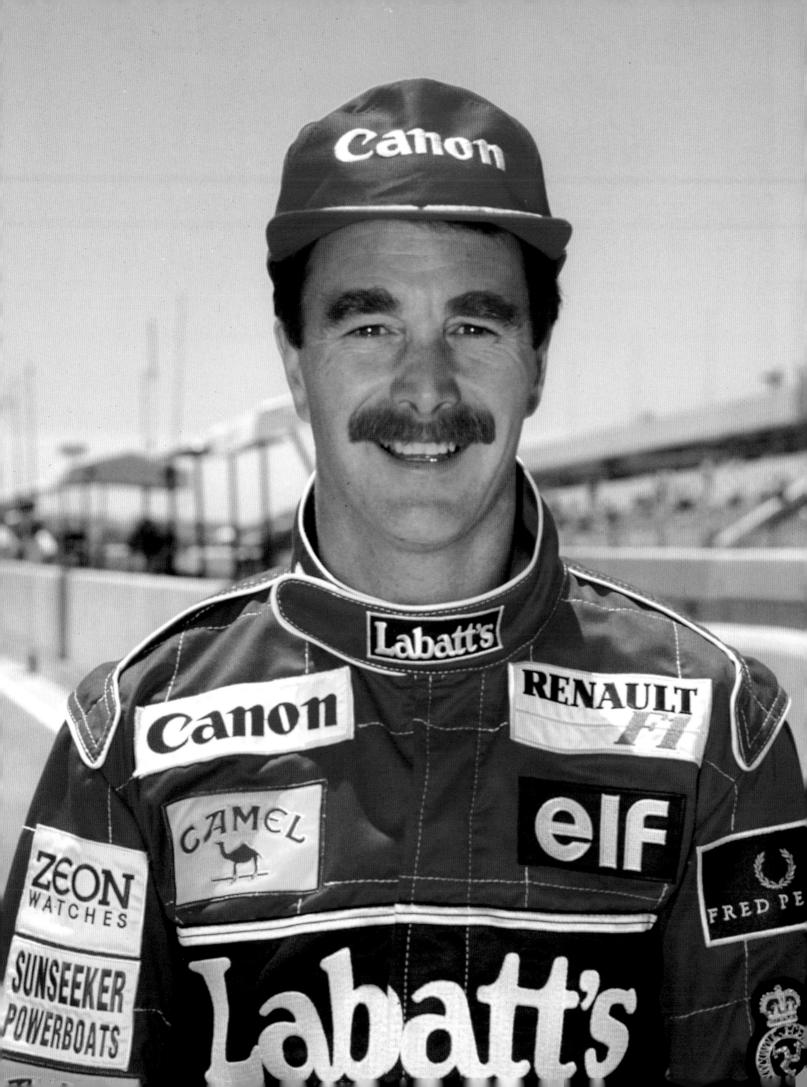

Index

Figures in *italics* refer to captions to illustrations